Guerrilla Tactics for Teachers

ANDREW FULLER

GUERRILLA Tactics for Teachers

THE ESSENTIAL **CLASSROOM MANAGEMENT** GUIDE

First published in 2024 by Amba Press, Melbourne, Australia
www.ambapress.com.au

© Andrew Fuller 2024

The moral rights of the author have been asserted.

All rights reserved. No part of this book may be reproduced or transmitted in any form or by any means, electronic or mechanical, including photocopying, recording or by any information storage and retrieval system, without prior permission in writing from the publisher.

Cover design: Tess McCabe
Internal design: Amba Press
Editor: Andrew Campbell

ISBN: 9781923116719 (pbk)
ISBN: 9781923116726 (ebk)

A catalogue record for this book is available from the National Library of Australia.

About the author

Andrew Fuller is a clinical psychologist and family therapist who specialises in resilience, brains, and learning strengths. Andrew works with schools, students, and parents across the world.

Andrew is an author of many books, including: *Neurodevelopmental Differentiation: Optimising Brain Systems for Learning*, *Your Best Life at Any Age*, *The A to Z of Feelings*, *Tricky People, Tricky Behaviours*, *Unlocking Your Child's Genius*, *Raising Real People*, *From Surviving to Thriving*, *Work Smarter Not Harder* and *Beating Bullies*.

Contents

Introduction 1

Chapter 1	Starting well: An opportunity for madness or serenity 3
Chapter 2	The 10 most powerful ways to manage classrooms 19
Chapter 3	Keeping your cool and your stuff together 27
Chapter 4	Managing tricky students and increasing motivation 35
Chapter 5	Gang leadership and guerrilla dynamics for teachers 69
Chapter 6	Wheeling and dealing 95
Chapter 7	Time making 101
Chapter 8	Curating great learning experiences 113
Chapter 9	Extracting miraculously good marks 129
Chapter 10	Keeping your head when all about you are losing theirs 147
Chapter 11	What do I do when students … 153
Chapter 12	The best guerrilla tactic of all 165

Introduction

A matador walks out to confront an enraged bull. The sun beats mercilessly down. The crowd yells support mixed with derision.

A netball player shifts her balance from one foot to the other. Delicately poised, she tenses her body to shoot for a vital goal. The jeering and cheering from the crowd are deafening.

A pilot flies over enemy territory, weaving and avoiding flak, and prepares for a dogfight.

A teacher wanders to the front of a class of rabid, feral kids. It's Friday afternoon, lunchtime has been wet and tense, there's a howling wind, and a full moon is rising.

Ha! There are days when teaching makes facing enemy gunfire, charging bulls, and the major league sports look like a walk in the park.

Successful teaching is about swashbuckling, feigning, acting, and swaying the crowd. It'd be enough to make your average pirate pale and run in the other direction.

Guerrilla Tactics for Teachers is about achieving more with less energy expenditure and much, much less stress. It is a compilation of ideas that I have researched, over years. It is the secret knowledge of survival in a business that loses many great teachers to other careers when they decide it is too hard and walk away.

This book is written in tough uncompromising language because having a sustainable career as a teacher requires tough clear-headed decision-making. At times it also requires ruthless prioritisation.

I know you have a dream. Possibly it involves eager students who are exploring new ideas, making amazing discoveries in collaboration with a teacher that they trust and admire. There will be moments like this.

Even those inspired and talented teachers with a passion for kids and learning will have days when it all seems too much. This book is written to help you sustain yourself so that you and your students can benefit from your passion, skill, and verve.

Teaching can be great fun too. At its best it's like running your own gang. A gang of sharp-witted, bright young people who will, with the assistance of your well-timed input, go on to improve the world. As Neil Postman once observed, "Children are the living messages we send to a time we ourselves will not see".

Let the vitality and the vigour of your own life act as a role model for them.

Chapter 1
Starting well:
An opportunity for madness or serenity

Learning involves trying in a focused and strategic manner. It is not a spectator sport. Learning almost always involves challenge. Finding ways to make challenges worthwhile is the art of student engagement.

Our brains are such greedy users of our energy that most of us like to conserve effort. Unless there is something new or exciting with considerable survival value going on, we tend to wander off. States of unfocused reverie are great for calm, creative insights, but effective learners have to be active participants in the process.

This is why the role of a teacher in a brain-aware classroom is a little like the conductor or arranger of a piece of music that engages the audience. How to raise or lower the tempo, where and when to place the crescendo, and where to position the refrain, are all essential. This is using neuroscience to intersect with the art of teaching.

Starting

You enter a classroom with all your senses tingling on high alert. Greeting students as you enter, you "read" the room. Who looks weary? Who avoids eye contact? Who is chattering and distracted? Who looks about to slump into a dispirited or comatose state?

Your aim is to convert the restless and the uninterested and inspire the motivated into a class of engaged, knowledgeable learners with a resilient mindset. This book aims to help you do this.

Stephen Covey rightly pointed out it is always a good idea to keep the end in mind. In other words, start the year in the way that you want it to end.

Let's start by talking about building good relationships with all the key players:

1. Getting to know your students
2. Getting to know their parents
3. Getting to know your colleagues
4. Getting to know yourself.

❶ Getting to know your students

For teachers to have a happy career, they need to get on well with the people they spend the most time with – their students. For this reason, your students are your number one priority.

When students are asked what sorts of teachers they like, boys say they like someone who is fair, who can control a class, and who can take a joke; girls say someone who is friendly and is personally interested in them.

From the first moment you meet them, hit the ground running with respect and dignity. Greet your students at the door when they come in. Be welcoming and upbeat. Model enthusiasm and excitement.

Greet students by name. Get to know the students fast! Make a game of trying to remember as many students' names as you possibly can.

On page 6 is a "Getting to know you" survey that you may like to use to get to know your students.

Several activities that you might like to use to help everyone in your class get to know one another are outlined below.

Bio poems

Start the year with a biographical poem. This might be a series of lines with each line beginning with a letter of their name and a digital photo for each student.

Pizza portfolios

Give each student a pizza box. The student decorates the box and writes his/her name on the top and each side. Throughout the year, students place pieces of work inside the box, creating a portfolio. This can be shared with visitors and parents. At the end of the year, they are able to take it home.

Time capsules

Begin the school year by creating time capsules with your students. Time capsules may include personal details such as their height, favourite foods, a handwriting sample, a timed math test (multiplication facts), some predictions (both individual and class), as well as resolutions. Wrap them in wrapping paper to seal them, then put them all into a large, taped box, kept in plain sight. Open it during the last week of the year.

"GETTING TO KNOW YOU" SURVEY

Name _____

1. What are your main interests?
   _____
   _____
   _____

2. I like school:
   ☐ Always ☐ Mostly ☐ Sometimes ☐ Occasionally ☐ Never

3. What we learn at school is interesting:
   ☐ Always ☐ Mostly ☐ Sometimes ☐ Occasionally ☐ Never

4. What time do you normally go to sleep on a week night? _____

5. What time do you usually wake up? _____

6. What do you usually eat for breakfast? _____

7. How many hours would you spend watching screens on a usual day? _____

8. How many hours would you spend playing computer games on a usual day? _____

9. How many hours do you spend messaging/in chat rooms/on apps on a usual day? _____

10. In a usual day at school is there a particular time of day you find it most difficult to concentrate? If yes, what time of day?
    ☐ Start of the day _____
    ☐ After morning break _____
    ☐ Just before lunch _____
    ☐ Just after lunch _____
    ☐ Towards the end of the day _____
    ☐ Other (please say what time) _____

11. I read books for pleasure on average (tick the answer that is true for you)
    ☐ Once a day ☐ Once a week ☐ Once a month ☐ Rarely ☐ Never

12. **Last question!** If you could learn more about anything you could think of, what would it be?
    _____
    _____

Thank you for doing this!!!

Birthday cards

Have students get to know each other by making birthday cards. They sit in groups and design a card for the person across from them. They have to find out what hobbies that person enjoys, books they like to read, games they like to play, places they have been, and design a birthday card accordingly.

The card should have the student's name, a greeting, and their date of birth. Keep the cards by the classroom calendar and post the birthdates. When someone's birthday comes up, the card gets passed around the room for everyone to sign. Give it to the birthday student on their special day along with a birthday pencil. Make up a half birthday for those who were born during the summer holidays. This makes handling birthdays much simpler. The kids love to read their cards.

Procedures

One of the easiest ways to get to know students is to start by creating procedures and delegating roles to students such as rotational classroom manager.

Get to know the kids and then give yourself six weeks to teach all the classroom procedures. Don't cram it all into the first week.

The sorts of procedures you might want to outline include:

1. How students enter the classroom
2. Activities when first entering the classroom (students should always do something that raises curiosity, piques interest, reinforces/reviews, or practises a skill, e.g., journal writing – DEAD TIME IS DEADLY TIME)
3. How to take the roll while students engage in some activity
4. How to obtain students' attention in 10 seconds or less

5. What signal will be used to get their attention and silence
6. What to do when it is necessary for them to use the toilets
7. What to do when a task or assignment is finished early
8. What to do when they have questions or want assistance
9. How papers will be collected and where to put them
10. How and when to move around the room
11. How to use classroom materials and where to find them
12. What to do when returning from an absence
13. How to get materials without disturbing others
14. How to discard papers without disturbing others
15. How to get ready for finishing a lesson
16. How the class will be dismissed (bell or teacher)
17. What object you are going to give students who are out of your class (one teacher I know has an old wooden toilet seat that is used as the pass to go to the toilet; others have an oversized bright key).

You don't need to solve all of these. Put them up and ask students to suggest solutions. They will often come up with better ideas than either you or I would be able to.

Some procedures that I like include:

Unnamed pieces

Tracking the owners of no-name papers can take up a lot of time You are a teacher, not a detective. Create a folder labelled "NO NAMES". Hang the folder on the wall with one of those clear plastic holders. Students will then always know where to look before coming to ask about missing assignments or feedback.

Starting a class

Have a clear procedure for starting a class. One teacher I spoke to has a fishbowl containing laminated fish. Each laminated fish has a student's name on it. She also has three small cardboard boxes: one with something of value in it, one with an ordinary object in it, and one with nothing in it. When the class is ready, one student selects a laminated fish with a student's name on it. If that person is ready, they get to pick a box; if they are not ready, another name is selected.

Give out stickers or stamps to students who look like they are working hard. Stickers and stamps work regardless of the age of the students.

Categories

This activity is great for getting students into different groupings within your class and can provide the basis for short, sharp group work.

Ask your class to separate quickly into the smaller groups that you are about to announce. For mixing purposes, you should alternate two-group splits with multi-group splits.

As soon as the groups have formed, give the participants some time to say hello to one another. Upon identifying each of the groups, move on to announce the next split.

Here are a few sample group categories (don't hesitate to make up your own):

- Everybody fold your arms. If your right arm is on top, get together with the right-armers. Left-armers do the same.
- What month were you born in?
- Clasp your hands together so that your fingers interlock. Separate according to the position of the thumbs, left or right on top, or other preference.

- How many children are in your family, including yourself?
- Which leg do you put into your pants first?
- What side of the bed do you get out of in the morning?
- What colour are your eyes?

You can also use these methods if you need two (or more) teams from a class. If you can't get an even split, simply move a few students.

Once you have these groupings, you can use different categories to do short, sharp group work.

On the page opposite is an activity called "Find someone who has ..." which can be used to help students get to know one another.

2 Getting to know their parents

As well as getting to know students, having clear lines of positive communication with parents early in the year pays off. Early and frequent contact with parents will help to nip any problems in the bud before they become real issues. It is worth the time, as it will save major time later!

Reaching out to parents pays off big time. Welcome them, acknowledge their role, and build a collaborative partnership. Parents who have not had the best experiences themselves at school will be the most important to reach out to.

Positive parental involvement is related to lower levels of behavioural problems and improved marks. If you want your life to be filled with less conflict and better academic outcomes, get to know your students' parents.

While building positive links with parents is easier in primary schools, it is probably even more important in high or secondary schools. Teenagers are a mystery even to themselves. Any group of people whose vocabulary has been pared back to "whatever", "as if", "like", and "don't know" is bound for trouble and confusion.

"FIND SOMEONE WHO HAS ..." ACTIVITY

(only one answer from each person)

- (A) Has visited a circus. *Which one?*
- (B) Knows the name of a local politician. *Who?*
- (C) Is a member of a sporting club. *Which one?*
- (D) Has been on television. *What show?*
- (E) Has been in a very dangerous situation. *What?*
- (F) Has done something wild on the spur of a moment. *What?*
- (G) Has visited an unusual place. *Where?*
- (H) Has found out something strange about their family's history. *What?*
- (I) Has a skill very few people know about. *What?*
- (J) Knows the meaning of their surname. *What?*
- (K) Has read a book that changed their life. *What?*
- (L) Has heard a piece of advice that was valuable. *What?*
- (M) Has been in a race. *What type?*
- (N) Has received an unexpected gift. *What?*
- (O) Has ridden a horse. *Where?*
- (P) Has sung in public. *Where?*

(A) Name	(B) Name	(C) Name	(D) Name
Which one?	Who?	Which one?	What show?
(E) Name	(F) Name	(G) Name	(H) Name
What?	What?	Where?	What?
(I) Name	(J) Name	(K) Name	(L) Name
What?	What?	What?	What?
(M) Name	(N) Name	(O) Name	(P) Name
What type?	What?	Where?	Where?

Make sure you have a list of parents' addresses, mobile phone numbers, and email addresses.

Send home postcards welcoming students and their parents to the year with you. Ask your students to design postcards that you can later use to post to parents, congratulating them on positive performances.

If your school permits it, send out a text message or email every Friday – just a brief update on the goings-on that happen each week. Include due dates and forthcoming events but also mention highlights.

As well as building a positive communication stream between yourself and the students' parents, it also helps family conversations. When parents ask what's been happening at school only to hear "Nothing", they can say, "Well, your teacher said you did …"

If something is spectacularly successful, you can even send a special text message so parents can surprise their kids at the dinner table that night with one of those comments like, "I got a text message from your teacher today, and she said …"

Parents overestimate their child's ability to manage their time. Some tasks you set to be done at home will have no time limits, but other tasks can be used to see how much a student can get done in 20 minutes.

Many parents don't feel welcome at school, so you will need to be the one who does the reaching out.

On the opposite page is a sample letter to parents (check with the school that they are happy for you to send this out before you put the letters in the post).

From time to time, disputes will occur with parents. When this occurs, it is useful to say to a parent something like: "Thank you for coming in today. I know that you are [insert their child's name]'s biggest supporter, so can I ask you to tell me about what is working out well for them." Then be prepared to listen and be silent.

LETTER TO PARENTS

Dear Mr/ Ms/Mrs ………

Hello! I am ……………'s teacher this year and I'm excited about having …………… in my class.

In the next few weeks, I will phone you to arrange a time to meet. In the meantime, there are a few things that I would like you to know. The most important of these is that I am committed to having a successful year for ……………… and to working with you to help make this happen.

There are a number of factors that help students succeed in school, and I want to make sure that …………… is "firing on all cylinders" at school.

1. Sleep. Research tells us that the best amount of sleep for students in school is between eight and nine and a quarter hours. Sleep-deprived children snooze rather than learn. Keeping computers, electronic games, and mobile phones out of bedrooms helps students get the sleep they need to succeed.
2. Breakfast is really important for brains. Try to ensure your child eats a healthy breakfast – ideally one with more protein and less sugar and carbohydrate.
3. There will be homework to do, usually about 20 minutes each night. If your child consistently says they have no homework, please contact me.
4. Work should be handed in on Wednesdays unless there are exceptional circumstances.
5. Too much time spent watching TV or playing computer games reduces success at school.

In the rush of a busy school day, contact by phone is not always easy. You might prefer to email me if you are wanting more information or if there is anything you would like me to know about ………… My email address is …………

If you could please email me a description of your child and how you feel they learn best, I would appreciate it.

I am looking forward to a great year working with you.

Sincerely

If you give parents a sense that they are truly listened to, they are more likely to consider your point of view in a calm way.

Sometimes parents will want to discuss matters at inappropriate times. Be very clear that while you are happy to speak to them, now is not a possible time. Then set up a time that works for both of you.

If you are scheduling meetings with parents, try to do it during recess, before school, or at lunch, so those meetings will have a definite end point. If you're meeting a parent after school, they know you're just going home afterwards, so they'll take as much time as they want, as opposed to as much time as you need.

3 Getting to know your colleagues

Be polite to cleaners, office people, and any maintenance staff. Along with the bus scheduler and the timetable, they run the school. The senior management team are also your colleagues. Talk to them if you have concerns. While many of them are very talented, only rarely can they actually read minds.

In great schools you will make a lot of contacts, work well with other professionals, expand your knowledge, and have a lot of fun. That doesn't mean you can't also be astutely aware of who you are working with.

Look at your colleagues. Know their nuances, preferences, how they perform under pressure, and who they are closest to at school. Your colleagues are your possible future. Really study them closely. Who is happiest? Who looks like they could be teetering on the edge of a nervous breakdown? Who looks 10 years older than their biological age? Who has the most fun?

One of the things worth knowing in organisations is that pessimists are the possessors of privilege. The people who have the most to lose are often the most pessimistic about any change.

Starting well: An opportunity for madness or serenity

These are the "world-weary warriors" who make comments like, "We tried that in 2023 and it didn't work then, and it isn't going to work now". Some of the music teachers can raise a smile. The mathematics department is full of standard deviants, the English teachers are all too often frustrated poets, and the social science/humanities staff are wayward souls.

Observe where they sit in the staff room. Is there a power table that teachers vie to sit at? Is there a social ladder that they are climbing up at the expense of others?

Most schools contain a few people who have become shipwrecked on the coastal fringes of life – marooned forever in a time warp called "school".

Look around and identify the guilt police. These are the tsk-tskers who take the moral high ground in the school. Make a clear decision at the outset: do you really want to impress these people? If you do, best of luck!

Be friendly to everyone. Be professional, but don't feel you need to be defined by them.

You can learn a lot about survival in a school by sitting back and watching for a while without any particular allegiance to any group.

You can also save yourself a lot of time and energy by working out whom you could collaborate with and talking to them about sharing workloads.

Your work colleagues are your work colleagues. As fun as I hope they are to be around, they are your work colleagues. They are NOT your substitute family, unpaid counsellor, favourite agony aunt, or potential next lover.

Keep a social life away from your work.

Getting to know yourself

Tell yourself each morning that you will make at least 12 big mistakes today. When you make them, feel bad for a moment but then remind yourself you are still within budget. In fact, think to yourself: "One down, only 11 to go for today."

You need to maintain a support team so that when the excrement hits the ventilation system it does not intrude into your life space. Have a still point in your life – a regular activity or time each week away from work to regather your wits.

Burnout is a risk in all careers but especially in those where there is contact with a lot of people, multiple demands, limited time, and sometimes little control over the pace of events. It is estimated that the average teacher has more interactions and decisions in a day than an air traffic controller.

Think about the following nine ways of making your life as a teacher and a human being a little easier.

1. Be a thief!

Steal, borrow, pinch, pilfer ideas, strategies, and approaches from your colleagues. Give credit where credit is due but steal all the same. People have great ideas. Use them. Don't ever be accused of re-inventing the wheel. Good teachers borrow ideas; great teachers steal them. Twitter for teachers is a good place to start. Instagram has enormous amounts of ideas, and on Facebook check out the Learning Strengths page.

2. Rituals

Have some rituals in your life each week that take you away from work: the Friday night pizza, netball on Tuesdays, the Wednesday evening swim, or the Sunday movie. Put them in your diary at the start of the year and remember that sticking to them matters.

3. Ask for help

This is really hard to do. Often, it seems far easier to just do it yourself than to explain how something should be done. Parents, school volunteers, friends, and students can be a valuable time-saving resource in your classroom, but only if you take the time to ask them. People can only feel involved if you give them something to be involved in.

4. Your job is impossible

Recognise it! Face facts. No one can be on top of everything all the time. Teaching is not a job that can be completed. It is an ongoing process.

5. Give up "busy" and "not bad"

You will be busy. At times you will be overwhelmed. Even so, pretend that you have enough time. You have as much time as everyone else – pretend that it is enough. Don't fall into the often-self-fulfilling trap of saying to yourself (or to others): "I'm so busy."

6. It's only an emergency if you are calling 000

There is a growing trend to treat everything as if it is important, essential, and an emergency. This leads some people to run schools in the same manner as a psychiatric crisis centre. We are there to teach the students. Some things that don't fall into the teaching/imparting knowledge category just may not be worth the amount of time and effort required.

7. Seek out a mentor

Some business leaders have four mentors and chat with one each week on a monthly basis throughout the year. You need at least one and maybe more. Retired teachers can be invaluable.

8. Keep a blue day book or file

Whenever you receive an acknowledgment or some lovely feedback, or a positive outcome, keep it in a file, because one day when the chips are down you are going to need to remind yourself of why you do this job. Let's face it: it's not for the international travel, exotic fashions, or wild parties!

9. Sleep

Teachers cannot function if they deprive themselves of sleep. If you are a beginning teacher, you will be amazed by how tired you will feel at times. Even experienced teachers will need to be careful to make sure they get enough sleep at report times and towards the end of each term.

Chapter 2

The 10 most powerful ways to manage classrooms

The long-term aim is *not* for you to manage student behaviour; it is for students to learn how to manage their own behaviour.

It is 2.30 on a Friday afternoon. There is a west wind blowing. A full moon is rising. You are facing a classroom of wild students. You are on a highway to hell.

These 10 strategies may well save a teacher's dignity, career, composure, and possibly even their sanity.

Create a sense of home

We are coming out of a difficult few years, and many people have been wounded and unsettled. It is time to move on. Three important factors in their recovery are safety, certainty, and belonging.

Having a place where you feel safe is necessary for development and learning to occur. If it is at all possible in your setting, lay claim to your own classroom. Of all of the ways to improve behaviour and increase learning in schools, having teachers "own" their classroom would top my list.

By nature, we are territorial creatures, and if we initially feel that we are entering someone's domain we are often on our best behaviour. Eventually, "ownership" of this space can be shared, but essentially students act best when they are welcomed into an adult-owned teacher space.

2 Culture beats programs

Classroom management and behaviour improve when we create kind and empowering school or classroom cultures based on relationships where people expect to treat others well and, in turn, be treated well themselves. Where they:

- **C** **Connect** with one another
- **P** **Protect** one another
- **R** **Respect** one another.

This takes schools and classrooms away from lengthy lists of rules, rewards, and consequences to a much more simple but effective principle: "Treat others as you would like to be treated yourself."

Well-being and behavioural standards are then conveyed through the culture of the school, with lessons taught as issues and opportunities arise. In addition, consider check-ins and well-being plans.

3 Here *everyone* gets smart (and you will get even smarter)

Improving your students' self-concept changes everything. Having your students know that you believe in them, that you think they are smart, and that with you this year they can get even smarter, improves their behaviour and learning.

Go to www.mylearningstrengths.com and begin by completing the analysis for yourself. You will be emailed a free letter outlining your top learning strengths and suggestions about how to use these to increase learning in other areas. Knowing your own learning strength profile will help you to see how you can help your students towards success.

Once you have an understanding of your own learning strengths, ask your students to complete the analysis (make sure they enter their correct email address!) and discuss the letter with them. For children younger than Year 4, parents may need to do it with them. For very young children, parents could complete it on their behalf and treat the results as a rough guide as they develop and mature.

You can repeat the analysis as many times as you like, but generally once every term or six months will be most useful.

A full report outlining a detailed pattern of learning strengths is available for $20. This report provides detailed strategies and a personalised learning plan.

 Develop pods

Not all students will change their behaviour because of a strongly positive school culture and a strengths-based approach to learning. A small group will need further assistance in the form of pods.

A pod is a group of three adults who between them care for the learning and emotional needs of a group of students as well as being the main link point for family liaison in high schools. Ideally the three teachers continue with the same group of students throughout their time at the school.

Most students will be able to relate to all three teachers. Some students, however, are unable to hear mixed news (praise as well as suggestions) from the one person. For these students we split the roles of the pod into:

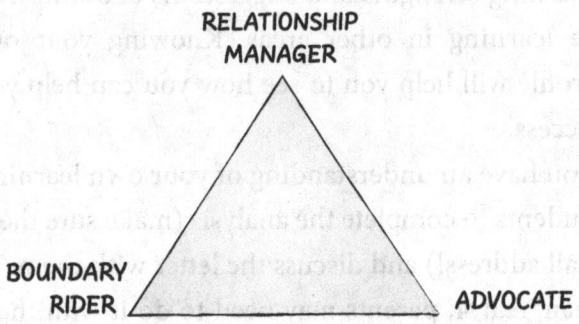

The boundary rider puts consequences in place. The advocate engages and supports the student and removes themselves whenever possible from disciplinary processes. The relationship manager oversees the process and has the final say in the event of professional differences about student management.

5 Run your gang

The most successful classrooms are run like gangs. The teacher is the head of the gang and welcomes members into his or her gang. Have routines. Let students know this is the way we do things here.

Gangs have lifecycles, and in Chapter 4 we will outline high-priority actions to manage classrooms at each cycle.

6 Get to know them and engage them

Greet them by their name at the classroom door. Signify to them that *they* are coming into *your* domain. The more that you can personalise the space, the better.

Invite parents to let you know about their child and when they learn best.

Be clear about your standards

Imagine you are an umpire in a grand final. The scores are close, it is the final quarter, and the players will do anything to create an advantage.

Do you think that giving meaningful looks, saying, "Excuse me, I'm waiting!" loudly, giving warnings, shaking your head, or looking disapprovingly before finally blowing the whistle and saying, "I've given you enough warnings!" will work? Well, you are in the equivalent situation every day. You need to be clear, fast, and decisive to get on with the game of learning.

Choose "which hills to die on" – don't react to everything. If something really pushes your buttons, react early. Don't wait till you are truly upset before dealing with it.

One of the most common mistakes some teachers make is not following through on consequences when students make poor choices. They tend to try the "ignore" tactic for way too long, hoping the behaviour will just go away, or they give too many chances ("If you do that again …"). Or they try to gain a confession ("Did you do …") or an immediate self-assessment ("Did you think that was a smart thing to do?").

This is based on a false belief that if a student gains insight into their own actions, they will change their ways. *No, they won't!*

These teachers threaten but don't follow through until they are frustrated and angry, and the consequence becomes a punishment delivered with too much emotion and a later sense of failure.

8 Build a culture of co-operation

Give more praise than punishment. Don't take students' behaviour personally. Students want you to like them. Praise them and increase the amount of feedback. The way to do this is to increase the number of statements you make that begin with "I noticed …"

9 Location, location, location

Every real estate agent knows it – location, location, location! Your proximity to students makes a difference to their behaviour. If you arrange the room so you have a barrier between yourself and your students, your chances of classroom control are zilch.

Use whispers and quiet comments to students as you move around the room rather than speaking across a room.

10 The best interventions are non-verbal

Improving behaviour in schools and classrooms occurs at a rate of one relationship at a time. While all kids play up from time to time and try to gain peer acceptance, almost all of your students won't be persistently difficult for people whom they trust, like, and admire.

At the start of the year, let your students know the warning signs that you are unhappy with their actions. For example, say, "Usually I will be writing in black or blue, but if I pick up the red pen you will know the entire class is about to get into some serious business unless your behaviour improves immediately."

Also introduce them to soft, coloured, two-sided tokens (e.g., red and yellow). Say to them: "If I place this in front of you with the red side up, you will know that unless your behaviour improves you will lose some of your next break. If I come back and turn it over to the yellow side, you will know that you are still on notice but as long as you keep behaving well you have regained your break time. If you want to dispute this, talk to me about it in your break. Lesson time is for learning."

Chapter 3
Keeping your cool and your stuff together

If at all possible, select a school that has close to a multiple of 300 students. For example, 300, 600, 900, 1200, or 1500 students. It seems that in schools of these population sizes there is enough administrative support and most teachers are teaching in the areas they want to teach in.

Sanity in schooling means being in charge of your own destiny. The first thing is to ensure that your students, their parents, and even your colleagues have a clear idea of what you are on about.

Imprinting and marketing a positive culture

You are in the marketing business. You are marketing to students about the desirability of learning and possibilities for themselves. You are marketing to parents about your own expertise and appropriate behaviours, attitudes, and educational methods. Trickiest of all, you are marketing to other teachers.

The key phases of constructing a positive culture in a classroom or a school are:

① Have *no more* than three coherent messages

For example, in my classroom we get smart, make friends, and have fun. Phrase your messages in positive terms. Human nature rebels against anything someone tells us not to do.

② Make small requests of students and parents early on

Making individual requests build cultures of co-operation. Asking a student "Would you mind helping me by …" allows them to feel important and involved and helps to create a positive relationship. If a student replies that they don't want to help you, don't convert a request into a demand. Instead, respond by saying "Oh, ok" and move on to ask another student. However, always come back to the first student you asked later on with another request. Even if you never get them to do anything, the message you want to convey is that their contribution is valued and you are not giving up on them.

③ Be a fantastic role model

People imitate the behaviours they see. Be upbeat, friendly, respectful, and interested in what you can learn.

We live in a world where young people have too few great models. Some of them are saturated in misery and negativity. Be the antidote. Believe in them. Teachers can be superb role models. Make sure that you are role-modelling how to have a great life and make positive changes rather than how to be an exhausted stress-head.

④ Use visual proximal prompts and reminders

Ask students to create a symbol or some posters to remind everyone in the class of the behaviours we want to have.

You might like to add some visual prompts of your own. Here are two examples:

Deadlines are CLOSER than you think	WARNING! Positive attitudes only past this point

⑤ Enlist public promises

Develop a contract with key statements about positive behaviours and gradually ask students to sign an agreement to be part of this.

⑥ Ensure you have routines

Procedures lead to habits lead to routines. Put your emphasis on classroom management rather than on discipline.

⑦ Schedule catchups

Allocate five minutes of every day to catch up with one student, one on one.

Working the crowd – schmoozing and cruising

To work the crowd effectively, you need to have control over where students sit and what groups they move into to complete different tasks.

Ideally, seating arrangements should be worked out for each week and by the end of each term most students will have sat together for some time.

Classroom layout

I know of no research that indicates that one classroom seating arrangement is better than another, but a few general principles are helpful.

This is a fairly typical classroom layout. The teacher's desk is at the front. The desks are lined up. Disruptive behaviours are most likely in the corner furthest away from the teacher's desk.

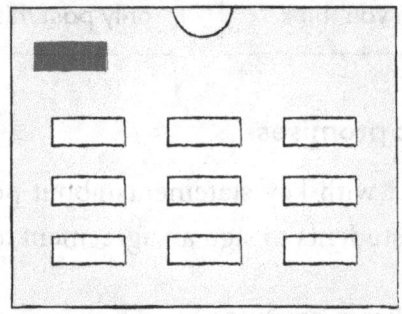

Generally, teachers find it valuable to push their desk against the wall or place it at the back of the room and to then arrange the students' desks in a fashion that suits their style. They then walk around the class and count their steps. The aim is to ensure that they can be in close proximity with as many students as possible in the least number of steps. Some other designs are:

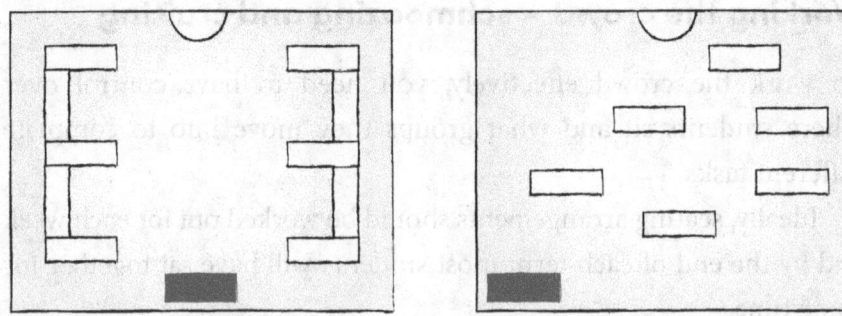

Personalise your space. This is your domain. The more environmental signifiers you have that indicate to students that they are coming into your domain, the better.

In secondary/high schools, do anything, plead, beg, pout, cast pathetic looks if you have to but get a classroom you can call your own and decorate it. Some teachers have taken this idea further and have adopted a corridor as well.

Each week give students a card with a symbol that matches the table they are to sit at as they enter your classroom. In secondary schools, you might allocate students to a table number as they arrive to your class.

Another way of shaping the class is to give students cards with different questions written on them as they enter the classroom, Label seats with the answers and ask students to sit at the seat that has the correct answer.

Short, sharp group work

Use the categories activity outlined in Chapter 1 (page 9) to form short, sharp groups. For example, you could say, "Please stand up and find your eye-tone friend [the student in the class with the most similarly coloured eyes] and tell them what you know about [fill in the gap]. On your way, say good morning to two other people."

You can use any types of groups (birthday friends, shoe friends, arm crossers, area friends, ear wrigglers, nose twitchers) for brief activities. These increase student engagement, are associated with improvements in marks, and also diversify the social connectedness of your class. Ideally, group activities of this type should only go on for a few minutes before students are asked to return to their seats.

Group sizes should generally be between two and five. The reason for these group sizes can be seen from the work of David Perkins below.

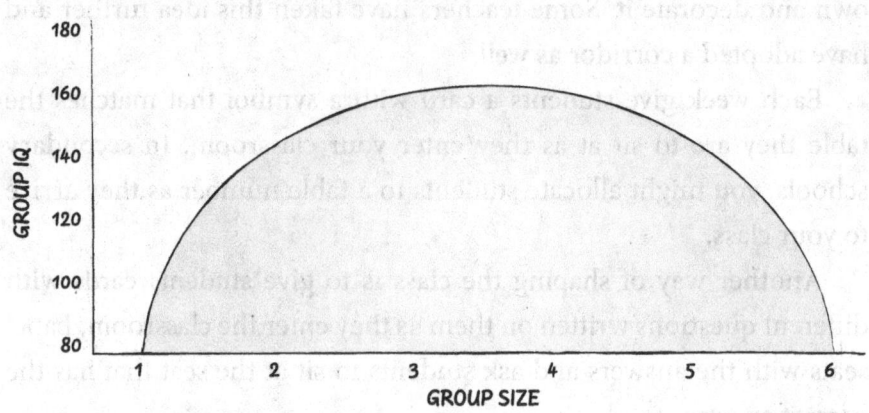

SOURCE: DAVID PERKINS, *KING ARTHUR'S ROUND TABLE: HOW COLLABORATIVE CONVERSATIONS CREATE SMART ORGANIZATIONS*, JOHN WILEY & SONS, 2003.

Student mailboxes

Consider buying an over-the-door shoe holder (the kind that has a pocket for each shoe) and hanging it on the wall of your classroom. Put pictures of your students on each pocket so they have their own mailbox. Put all their papers that need to go home in their mailboxes, and it will be their responsibility to check their box before they leave. You can also use this as a way of communicating one-on-one with students.

Noise

If the class gets too noisy, switch off all the classroom lights and fans. Once the students find that the room has suddenly turned dim, they will look around them. When they see you at the light switch with your finger on your lips, they will know that they have been making lots of noise and it's time to be quiet and carry on with their task. Don't do it too often!

Another idea is a "noise thermometer" that looks like a one-metre-tall thermometer with red Velcro representing the mercury. Number the scale from zero (no noise) to 10 (extreme noise/out of control). The thermometer starts at zero each morning. When the class gets louder, raise the thermometer to a level that matches their noise level. You never have to say a word. Usually, when students see you near it, the room immediately becomes quieter! If it hits five, the class loses two minutes off recess, and as it is raised even higher, they lose more time.

Painted windows

For those of you who are artistic and would like to make your classroom look exceptionally alive, select a major theme and paint the window glass with regular tempera paints mixed with liquid soap. This allows the paint to be easily washed off when you are ready to change themes. These paintings create a vibrant colour wash in the room and are absolutely incredible.

RATE YOUR CLASSROOM'S LEARNING ENVIRONMENT

(place a tick or a cross in each box)

- [ ] My classroom is lit by natural or broad-spectrum lighting.
- [ ] I use movement and teamwork to improve learning outcomes.
- [ ] My classroom is maintained at 18–24 degrees Celsius.
- [ ] My classroom lights can be dimmed as well as brightened by dimmer switches or curtains.
- [ ] Noise is dampened so people can hear by mats or carpets.
- [ ] The canteen serves brain-friendly food.
- [ ] Most students (and staff) get adequate sleep (at least 8 hours).
- [ ] My classroom looks different through colour and decoration.
- [ ] I have a classroom I can call my own.
- [ ] Students are encouraged to drink water throughout the day.
- [ ] The importance of breakfast and nutrition is emphasised as a way of enhancing learning.
- [ ] The classroom feels good to be in.
- [ ] Music is used at times in my classrooms as well as around the school.
- [ ] Aromas such as lemon, rosemary and basil are used in my classroom.

Chapter 4
Managing tricky students and increasing motivation

*"The problem is not that there are problems.
The problem is expecting otherwise and thinking that
having a problem is a problem."*
– Theodore Rubin

John Lennon once sang, "Instant karma's gonna get you", and teaching is a profession that has instant karma. Teachers get back what they give out.

Any classroom contains a variety of characters. It will take you a bit of time to learn their idiosyncrasies, but reading your crowd and shifting your strategies accordingly pays off – big time.

Key principles for engaging difficult students

1 Every day is a clean slate

Forget what happened yesterday. Students can be unpredictable, lively, and enlightening. Enjoy each of them each day without holding their mistakes of the past against them.

2 Be flexible

People who are flexible don't get bent out of shape. Go with the flow in your lessons. Students will bring their own perspectives, so let those guide your discussions.

3 Never use sarcasm

Most kids don't understand it. All they get is a sense that you are being nasty.

4 Always try to let students save face

If you have had a negative interaction, within 10 minutes find a way to ask them a question they know the answer to.

5 Be prepared to give your best-laid plans the flick

Don't be afraid to set aside the carefully planned-out lesson if you realise that something else needs to be addressed first. Be aware of the needs of your students.

6 Don't take everything personally

When a student is being defiant, annoying, or whatever, try to tell yourself that there is some reason for the misbehaviour. If you address the underlying issue, you can avoid a lot of behaviour. Take your sail out of their winds.

7 Don't assume students know what you are thinking (or feeling)

Many young people are not good at reading social cues. Be clear and explicit. Be prepared to say to students something like: "If you keep doing that, I'm likely to get annoyed. When I get annoyed, not only does my head spin around but green bile shoots out of my mouth, the walls get covered, and dreadful things happen – dreadful things that are possibly unimaginable to you. Be careful!"

8 Keep a joke book

This can be used to break up the odd tense moment.

9 Use the power of the whisper

Never shout – you'll have nowhere to go. Well-paced whispers are always best. Follow these up with quiet discussions on the side with unruly students.

Never get into arguments or debates with a student in front of the rest of the class. As soon as that happens, the student will do what he or she can to avoid losing face in front of the rest of the class, and that usually means an escalation of the problem. Find a way to say, "You obviously have a point to make that is very important to you, but we need to continue with [whatever it is the class is doing]. Let's talk about this after class."

For example, go quietly up to a student who is distracted and say, "I am frustrated when you talk loudly in my classes. This distracts others and stops them from learning. Work quietly or you have to work alone – you decide."

Also, don't punish the whole class for the actions of a few. This only builds resentment and an "us versus them" attitude.

If a student is not working, you might consider quietly telling them that if they don't want to do the tasks you have set they will have to clear it with their parent(s) first. Ask them to decide whether you should call their parents to get their OK or whether they're going to choose to do the work.

10. Always follow through

If you have specified a consequence for a behaviour, make sure you follow through. Don't threaten punishments when you are angry. You might say, "There will be a consequence for this" and then give yourself time to consider what that will be.

Don't threaten a consequence you can't follow through on. It is always better to give yourself and the student time to calm down before deciding what consequence is appropriate.

11. Not every battle has to be won

Don't be a control freak. You don't have to "die on every hill". Students can get great entertainment from sneering, rolling their eyes, burping, snorting, and generally being provocative. If you take the bait, it will be "game on".

In the heat of the moment, step back and ask yourself, "In the grand scale of things, how much is this worth?"

In communicating a concern, it is better to firmly focus on the behaviour: "I hear burping from the back – I suggest you get on with your work."

12. Nip it in the bud

For thousands of years, teaching has occurred through a cunning mix of fear, distraction, and bribery. Use these tools. When things look nasty, also use your group formations (shoe friends, etc.) to move kids around.

Spend more time focusing on the behaviours you do want to see than the behaviours you don't want to see. To change behaviour, increase the amount of praise (at least four positive comments for each suggestion) and also increase the number of opportunities your students have to contribute and respond.

13 Catch them being good

Don't just catch students when they behave inappropriately – catch them being good as well, and acknowledge this.

14 Set very clear boundaries

Have a few, clear rules that everyone in your class knows.

Behaviour is not just about behaviour

The moods that your students experience aren't just to do with whatever is happening that day. They also have a lot to do with the chemicals running around in their brains and bodies.

Behind learning and behind behaviour are brains. Brains are run by neurochemicals.

The invisible world of body and brain chemistry has as much power to shift emotions as does a happy or sad event. When teachers hear this, they often heave a sigh of relief. It explains why some behaviours come "out of the blue" without any warning or causative event.

While teachers don't need to become experts in neurochemistry and neuroscience, there are a few key brain chemicals that are well worth knowing about. This knowledge has the power to change your classroom.

Reading the class

Almost every classroom contains four main groups:

1. High-fliers
2. The not-switched-on
3. The switched-off
4. CAVE-dwellers.

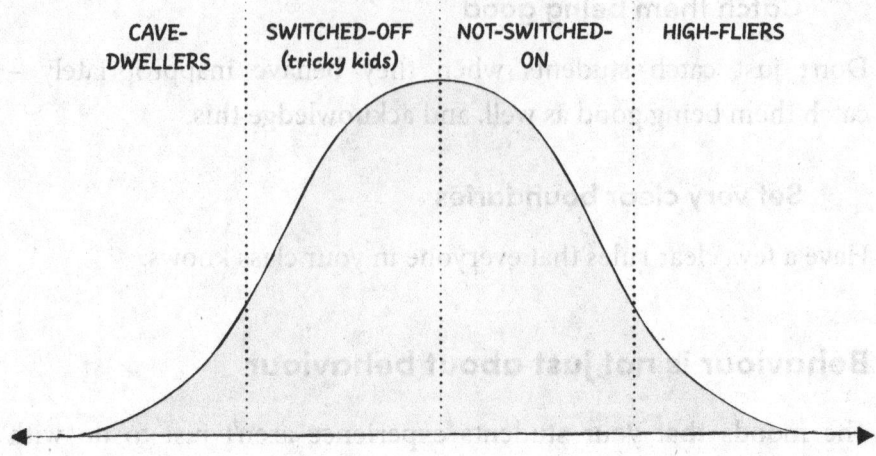

The proportions of each group in your class will vary according to what you do and how you engage them. Let's talk firstly about identifying them and engaging them in learning.

① The high-fliers

These are the dreamboat students, the students who learn, hand in work on time, create barely a murmur, and are compliant, lovable, and agreeable. Great kids, but sadly this group also contains your least resilient learners. Some of them are prone to perfectionism and won't try new challenges unless they are sure they are going to do well. While they will rarely, if ever, have behavioural problems, they need to be engaged to take on new challenges. Having lots of quizzes, guessing games, Fermi questions (questions that seek a fast, rough estimate of quantity that is difficult or impossible to measure directly), and problem-solving tasks really benefits these students.

② The not-switched-on

The light is on, but there's no one home. These students have learned that schools may reward the quiet non-thinker who slips beneath the radar. These are the kids who prompt you to ask yourself at the end of some days: "Was X here today?" These students are passengers rather than participants. Sometimes they perfect the art of invisibility. They are also your highest priority.

Changing students from not-switched-on to switched-on gives you a critical mass of pro-learning students. In many classrooms the line between a teachable and a non-teachable class is very narrow – I'd estimate about 7% of the class size. Therefore, your first task after identifying how many students you have in each of these groups is to work out activities that will engage these students.

3 The switched-off

These are the behaviourally difficult, tricky students. They are noisy, restless, and distractible, and they can take your energy and convert it into slush. You can devote your life to trying to engage the switched-off students in your class. The problem is: you are not their role model. Their peers are their role models. If they can win accolades from their peers by upsetting you, they will do it. Nothing personal. It's just business as usual for them.

Switched-off kids aren't necessarily troubled. They don't always have a problem, and they certainly aren't stupid. They want the approval of their peers. If the majority of their peers are saying "Ssshhh, this is fun" or "Stop mucking around, I want to do this", *some* of them will change sides and become switched-on students. This is why engaging the not-switched-on students is so important. Having control of seating arrangements and also being able to use flexible groupings for short, sharp group work are essential to containing and hopefully eventually engaging these students.

It's always worth taking five minutes out of each day to catch up with a student one on one. These students will initially be different with you one on one than in front of their peers. Be patient.

CAVE-dwellers

These are the Citizens Against Virtually Everything.

These students require individually tailored interventions that are beyond the scope of this book. For these students, call in the cavalry. Get as much support, professional input, and assistance as you can lay your hands on.

Plan your campaign of creating a positive classroom culture with as much care as a general planning a military encounter. Use every tool that you can muster in this campaign: praise, feedback, knowing the parents, building individual relationships, specialist support, and neurochemistry.

Types of tricky kids

 Rabbits in the headlights

These students master the art of invisibility. They go missing in action. You won't hear a murmur from them. They won't talk for long periods. They won't ask for help, ask questions if they are confused, or offer answers. Wide-eyed, they shun the spotlight and cringe if picked out from the crowd.

One of the oldest parts of the brain called the basal ganglia are likely to be in overdrive. This is often experienced as vigilance, anxiety, and feelings of being overwhelmed. The neurochemical surging through their brains that we want to lessen is cortisol.

The key to engaging the invisible worriers is to lower cortisol and the level of activity in the basal ganglia.

These things may help:

- Take your time – if you rush things, they will clam up.
- Develop calm repetition in the classroom.

- Have clear messages that this is the way we do things in this classroom.
- Have "no mistakes" times when we just play with ideas and concepts.
- Remind them when they learn something new about how it relates to things they have already accomplished.
- Use meditation and focusing activities:
  - Mindfulness
  - Theatre sports
  - Rhythmic activities
  - Hand-warming
  - Biofeedback games
  - Concentration and memory games.

Mistakes are opportunities for growth.

Shame causes low motivation. It is better, some students reason, to opt out than to endure humiliation.

Learning should be more about questions and less about answers. Many people learn more from their failures than their successes. Use guesstimation games, quizzes, puzzles, mazes, mysteries, forensic clues, and problem-solving games to build a resilient mindset. Ask students to give you a wrong answer and to tell you one reason they think it might be wrong.

2 Outbursters and argumentative kids

Dispute? Complain? These students will complain until the cows come home.

The part of their brain that is running hot is the anterior cingulate gyrus. These students often have laser brains – they get so focused on an idea or a dispute that they can't let it go. They don't know when to stop. They develop "brain-lock".

Because they get brain-locked, they really don't know how to let things go. Their levels of anxiety can be fiercely directed at having a battle with you. This means that if you don't change their direction, they will battle on and on. At the first instance of a dispute, gently move these students.

The "outbursters" are often quite high on adrenaline and dopamine. They can be highly motivated, especially when it comes to battles of wills.

These students can hold grudges for a long, long time.

If you assert that the moon is blue, they adamantly will say it is greenish. If you say, "You always seem to argue with me", they'll reply, "No I don't!"

The main way to engage outbursters is to lower their level of adrenaline while utilising their dopamine.

Movement is critical to engaging these students. They get so locked in mentally that unless they have a physical shift they don't change.

Other strategies include:

- Outdo your own argument
- "Find what is wrong with this information" games
- Puzzles
- Spot the error
- Challenges and personal bests.

These tricky students are vulnerable to getting stuck. Their ideas go around and around in repetitive loops. Their behaviours are often repetitive. To shift these students, it is desirable to alter the scene, timing, and content of the dispute.

3 Slugs

These students can be like sloths – they don't do much, they don't say much, they don't move much. They appear motivationally deficient.

Despite their low energy for learning, some of them manage to muster enough energy to be the court jesters.

The key to engaging the listless do-nothings is to use activities that raise dopamine – social interaction.

The neurochemistry of working with tricky students

Two brain chemicals teachers would usually like to see less of:

- Adrenaline
- Cortisol.

Two brain chemicals teachers would usually like to see more of:

- Dopamine
- Serotonin.

The big message here is: *You can't change behaviour until you have changed neurochemical balance.*

When students are stressed or threatened, the full repertoire of human behaviours are not on the shelf for them to select from. They won't just become agreeable by you saying, "Cheer up and get on with your work." You will need to think about how to shift their neurochemical balance.

Over the next few pages, we will cover how to discern and alter neurochemical balance. It is important for you to keep this information for your own use. For example, it could be extremely unwise for you to share with a parent something like, "I think your child is low on dopamine or serotonin."

Adrenaline

Adrenaline = Action – all pumped up with nowhere to go.

Adrenaline is at least partly responsible for the revved-up, "red-cordial" high. Living on adrenaline energy causes people to burn the candle at both ends. It makes people less flexible, and it makes it harder for students to change their moods.

When there is a lot of adrenaline, the amygdala (the fight-flight area of the brain) is very active. This is the part of the brain that works to defend against threats or tells you to run away from them. In fact, this part of the brain can get so active that it takes over almost everything else. It is very powerful.

You might know this yourself. Perhaps you've had a day where someone in the morning has said something to you that was mean or nasty and you just haven't been your usual self for the rest of the day. That is at least partly because you were threatened, and your adrenaline levels were raised, and your fight-flight response was activated.

Once a student gets an adrenaline rush, trying to change their behaviour is a complete waste of time until you've lessened the amount of adrenaline.

Signs that a student is having an adrenaline rush include driven behaviour or the "I gotta have it" attitude, difficulty getting to sleep, lots of energy, silly "hyper" behaviour, running off in an upset state, or lots of conflict and disagreement.

Having classrooms where a lot of repetition and rituals occur can lessen adrenaline. Giving an adrenaline-affected student a clear calm message that this is the way we do things in this class helps them to feel safe. Less stimulation such as quiet times can also help.

Every so often you might want to increase the amount of adrenaline, because it is an energiser. One way to do this is time trials. Consider purchasing an audible timer like those you see in hairdressers or use the timer on an interactive whiteboard.

ADRENALINE
Wired, revved-up, chatty, frazzled

When depleted

- Difficulty getting to sleep
- Lots of energy
- Storms off if upset
- Squabbling and bickering
- Restless and jumpy
- Reluctant to try new things
- Lots of busyness but not much gets done
- More talkative than usual
- Less flexible and more rigid
- Amygdala is activated
- Demanding.

What teachers can do

- Start fast (at their level)
- Give options, ideally visually – e.g., "Is it this ... or this ... ?"
- Pair responding with movement – e.g., "Stand up if you think ..."
- Use focusing activities such as "Try to clap your hands at the same instant I do" (harmonises and connects group, increases concentration)
- Slowly decrease the tempo – e.g., "Please sit down, turn to the person next to you and tell them ..."
- If they are unable to settle, go back to being active and then re-settle later.

SOURCE: ANDREW FULLER (2024). *GUERRILLA TACTICS FOR TEACHERS*. AMBA PRESS.

Cortisol

Cortisol is the other main neurochemical and hormone worth watching out for. Cortisol is the stress hormone, and it gets released with adrenaline. Terrific, huh? Stressed and revved-up!

Cortisol lowers language functioning. Have you have ever been shocked speechless where you temporarily couldn't put your thoughts into words? What was happening was that cortisol flooded into the Broca's area of your brain (the language production centre), shutting it down for a time. Students who are under lots of stress often have great difficulty putting their thoughts into words. That's why you sometimes get monosyllabic grunts, especially if they are teenagers.

Cortisol lessens students' ability to change tack. It makes them snappy and easily rattled. It also reduces the ability to filter irrelevant information, which partly explains why students who are stressed can find it difficult to prioritise. This is why note-taking systems are important.

Cortisol can also disrupt declarative memory (being able to say what you know about something) and can lower motivation levels in boys on tasks that do not involve rewards.

Signs that your students have elevated levels of cortisol include being worried and watchful, easily upset, on edge, easily tired, non-communicative, unusually defensive, and over-reacting to things.

Teachers often want to lessen the amount of cortisol in their classrooms and instead to have a calm and happy life. Alongside routines and rituals, making students feel safe from violence, ridicule, or humiliation lessens cortisol. Ensuring that kids do not have too much sugar and that they drink enough water also helps to reduce cortisol.

Getting enough sleep lowers both adrenaline and cortisol. Fluorescent lighting has been associated with elevated levels of cortisol. Switch them off whenever you can.

CORTISOL
Stressed, wary, reluctant

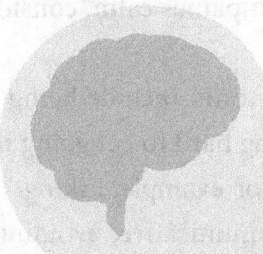 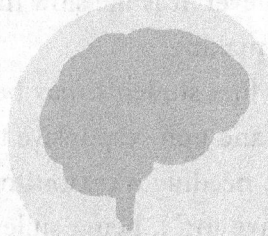

When depleted

- Difficulty expressing or articulating thoughts
- Worried and watchful
- Easily upset
- Prone to stomach upsets, headaches, and pains
- Defensive
- Overly reactive
- Pessimistic – predicts negative outcomes
- Finds it difficult to prioritise
- Affects memory (why teens under pressure can't explain actions).

What teachers can do

- Rituals at the start of classes
- Group problem solving – e.g., Fermi questions
- Phone a friend
- Realise memory may be decreased so reinforce key ideas
- Only require minimal responses for some students (for a time)
- Colouring in, drawing, create a mind map or concept map, complete mazes
- Request they drink water
- Give me a wrong answer and let's see if we can work out why it is wrong
- Turn mistake-making into thrill-seeking.

SOURCE: ANDREW FULLER (2024). *GUERRILLA TACTICS FOR TEACHERS*. AMBA PRESS.

Serotonin

Serotonin is the most powerful antidepressant known to humankind.

While dopamine gives you the pumped-up high, serotonin is the quiet achiever. It is the slow high and accompanies calm, considered decision-making.

Signs that students may be low on serotonin include being hard to please and non-responsive to praise, being hard to get going in the morning, needing a reason to do things (for example, asking "Why do we have to?"), being sullen and incommunicative, avoiding eye contact, and wanting to disappear from family activities. Low levels of serotonin are also linked to depression.

Serotonin can be increased by exercise. Whereas activities with repetitive movements particularly increase dopamine, exercise of almost any kind will raise levels of serotonin.

Giving positive, warm feedback also increases serotonin, as does giving students some choice and control through the use of rubrics.

Some students lead very pressured lives. Having times of the week in your class called "brain breaks" when the pressure is off – when they do an activity as they please and at the rate they choose – makes a contribution to serotonin levels.

Sleep is a big serotonin builder.

Too much caffeine and artificial sweeteners such as aspartame are toxic to serotonin. Try keeping students away from these.

SEROTONIN
Happy, calm, enjoyment

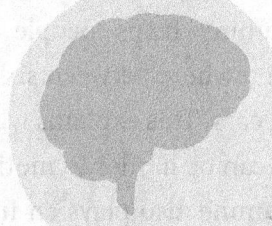

When depleted	What teachers can do
• Harder than usual to get going in the morning • Immune to praise • Everything seems to be a bother • Sullen, sad, or depressed • Needs a reason to do things • Avoids eye contact • Unwilling to participate in activities.	• Greet each student positively • Know something about their background, family, or interest areas • Tell them they are smart (and with you, this year, they will get even smarter) • Ask for their suggestions and opinions • Give great feedback (two things you really like and the next step is ...) • Build and cross-fertilise their learning strengths using neuro-developmental differentiation • Ask them to help others.

SOURCE: ANDREW FULLER (2024). GUERRILLA TACTICS FOR TEACHERS. AMBA PRESS.

Dopamine

Dopamine is the switched-on, pumped-up state. Dopamine is good for pleasure and motivation. It's the party animal of the neurochemical world.

Dopamine helps people change moods. It approaches adult levels somewhere between six and nine years then lowers during the teenage years. This explains why upper primary and junior secondary students can be harder to motivate.

Dopamine also plays an important role in shifting and directing attention and concentration.

There is some evidence that some families may have patterns where they have difficulty shifting from focusing on one activity to another. In these families there is a need to increase dopamine levels to help with this.

Signs that students have low dopamine include loss of motivation, being lethargic and tired, seeming uninterested and unwilling to have a go, and not being proud of achievements.

Teachers often want to increase dopamine. Several things help to do this:

- Sports that involve repetitive movements, such as table tennis, swimming, down or hand ball, percussion, body maths, volleyball, and brain gym
- Solving challenges and problems – puzzles, quizzes, Fermi questions
- Social interaction – short, sharp group work
- Rewards – inducements, bribery, call it what you will – it works!
- Dietary supplements of tyrosine and omega 3 and 6 have also been associated with increases in dopamine.

DOPAMINE
Energised, goal directed, motivated

When depleted

- Difficulty focusing
- Unmotivated
- Not proud of accomplishments
- Listless, lethargic, and tired
- Uninterested and won't try things out
- Finds it unsettling or difficult to shift from one activity to another
- Hard to please
- Grumpy, sullen, and uncommunicative.

What teachers can do

- Challenges, quizzes, puzzles (make some non-verbal)
- Group voting – e.g., "Stand up if ..."
- Increase social interactions
- Decrease screen time
- Make goals achievable and surpass them
- Positive feedback
- Humour
- Acknowledge each student's contribution
- Identify and build on learning strengths
- Use repetitive, rhythmic movement activities.

SSOURCE: ANDREW FULLER (2024). *GUERRILLA TACTICS FOR TEACHERS.* AMBA PRESS.

A tool for assessing the likely levels of each neurochemical in difficult-to-engage students is outlined on the opposite page. Give students a score of 0 to 3 (where 3 = very often, 2 = sometimes, 1 = occasionally, and 0 = rarely) for each of the statements from (a) to (e) for each of the neurochemicals: dopamine, cortisol, adrenaline, and serotonin. This will give you a total number in each box somewhere between 0 and 15. A high score in dopamine and serotonin indicates a need to increase those neurochemicals in the students. A high score in cortisol or adrenaline indicates a need to decrease those neurochemicals.

As a general rule of thumb, we want to increase dopamine and serotonin in our students and reduce cortisol and adrenaline.

Increasing motivation

Motivation is a slippery customer. Just when you want to rely on it, it puts its feet up, takes a few days off, and generally wants to be about as active as a sloth on long-service leave. Your "get up and go" has "got up and gone".

A slightly potted history of motivation

Originally motivation was a straightforward thing. People had drives and needs and conducted cost–benefit analyses and depending on the balance sheet either were motivated or lay around doing as little as possible.

That neat (but misleading) theory was upset when people inconveniently started hurling themselves into burning buildings to save people they didn't even know. It also didn't help when Harry Harlow, after rewarding his monkeys for months to solve puzzles, found the monkeys kept on playing even when the rewards stopped.

THE NEUROCHEMISTRY OF STUDENT ENGAGEMENT

Think of a few students you are currently experiencing difficulties engaging and rate them (3 = very often, 2 = sometimes, 1 = occasionally, 0 = rarely) for each of (a) to (e) below, then put the total for each neurochemical in the box.

Dopamine
(a) Difficult to get them focused on the task at hand
(b) Don't seem motivated to achieve goals
(c) Don't appear proud of accomplishments
(d) Seem lethargic and tired
(e) Uninterested and won't have a go

Total score ☐

Cortisol
(a) Reluctant to ask questions or raise their hands when they don't know something
(b) Have difficulty stating what they have learned
(c) Are "precious" about where they sit in class
(d) More smelly than usual
(e) Seem worried and watchful

Total score ☐

Adrenaline
(a) Lots of chattering
(b) Lots of conflict and disagreement
(c) Reluctant to try things that involve changes
(d) Lots of silly behaviour
(e) The classroom has a sense of busyness without much actually getting done

Total score ☐

Serotonin
(a) Avoid eye contact – seem to want to "disappear" in class
(b) Sullen and uncommunicative
(c) Hard to get going in the morning
(d) Hard to please – not responsive to praise
(e) Ask you "Why do we have to do this?" or "Is this in the exam or test?"

Total score ☐

High scores indicate you should consider altering their neurochemical balance.

Deci and Ryan in 2000 tried to steady the ship by pointing out there were actually two types of motivation: intrinsic and extrinsic. Intrinsic motivation – or doing things pretty much because you wanted to or found them fun – got a big tick of approval, especially in schools.

Related to this was the idea of "flow", discovered by the wonderfully named Mihaly Csikszentmihalyi, where people in a state of flow become completely absorbed in an activity for its own sake. Extrinsic motivation or doing things because of the payoffs (holidays, fame and glory, or driving sportscars to nightclubs with glamorous partners) was generally frowned upon. This was, of course, despite most teachers feeling that their salary levels were, justifiably, part of the reason they went to work in the first place.

Students don't behave like budding economists and states of flow are hard to regularly create in classrooms.

Why motivation matters (a lot) to teachers, parents and students

Schools, parents, and students undertake one of the most ambitious missions known to humanity. People have a hard time pushing themselves to do difficult things and an even harder time continually pushing themselves to improve over time.

Gaining a useful understanding of how brain learning and motivation work, and how to increase them, is among the most useful pieces of knowledge anyone can have.

Trying to make sense of all of this brings us to the neurochemical dopamine.

Dancing with dopamine

Neuropsychological studies have regularly shown that higher levels of dopamine equal increased motivation.

The main dopamine pathways in the brain include (non-neuro-nerds look away now!):

1. **The mesocortical limbic pathway** – transports dopamine from the VTA to the nucleus accumbens and amygdala and relates to feelings of being rewarded, motivated, or desiring or craving something
2. **The nigrostriatal pathway** – a pathway that links our midbrain and forebrain and gives us the impetus to move towards things that we want.

Essentially there are two aspects of the dopamine circuit:

1. **The seeking system.** Dopamine is increased when we anticipate and seek out something new.
People are on the hunt for new stuff all the time. Social media is a great example of this. It provides new ideas and also new social approval. It is also why we are fascinated by gossip and the news.
Dopamine is the neurochemical of desire. Desire starts to exist when you believe that doing something will result in pleasure, fulfilment, or satisfaction.
2. **The reward system.** Dopamine also increases when we experience little "wins", when tasks are completed, when we can tick things off a checklist or to-do list, or when personal goals are achieved.

Much of human exploration has been driven by dopamine. Let's go and check out what's happening over there – that looks interesting.

How to make yourself *really, really, really* want something

Neuro-craving is when your brain desires an outcome and, when it is finally achieved, your brain gives you a "hit" of dopamine. One example is cleverly arranged into music. Great songs create a tension in the listener that is resolved when a missing chord or note is sounded. The listener gets a hit of dopamine and wants to hear the song again.

You can increase dopamine through small changes in what you do with rapid and long-lasting results. Knowing how to leverage dopamine gives you a substantial 40% advantage in motivation.

Dopamine is more about wanting than having, whereas serotonin is more about having than wanting. When we feel excited or anticipate a good event, dopamine increases between 30- and 40-fold.

The first way to develop a dopamine "want" is to identify the edge, the new aspect of whatever you are learning or doing. If you can find something that intrigues you, you've already picked up your levels of motivation.

Having some caffeine increases dopamine release in the brain by about 30%.

Just thinking about what you want increases motivation by 50%, and writing down your goals even more so.

Computer games are beautifully designed to keep players entranced and on a dopamine edge. However, after playing for an extended period, most gamers are washed out.

Learn to spike dopamine by making the effort and the progress you make towards an outcome into a challenge. Focusing on the little goals along the way keeps dopamine flowing.

Downsides of dopamine

With dopamine there are no peaks without troughs. Many athletes have a glum period after winning a championship, and musicians often find the time that they spend at home after a successful tour to be difficult.

If we tap into a reliable source of dopamine, we tend to become obsessed with it. Phones, social media, and computer games are just some examples.

We all need to be careful to vary our sources of dopamine, because tapping into the same source repeatedly becomes a habit over time and risks turning into a raging addiction.

Having high levels of dopamine feels great but it also resets our baseline for what we consider to be fun and pleasurable. Try to appreciate the small things in life as well as the big wins.

If we seek out dopamine at high levels too much, we invite gloomy despondency into our lives. The great "high" of dopamine is that we feel pumped, but when the dopamine lessens or the source becomes unavailable for a time, we slump and find life boring and meaningless. The Greek poet Hesiod was onto this when he suggested, "All things in moderation".

A subtle but nasty downside of dopamine is that for every bit of dopamine that's released, there's a crash associated when prolactin is released in your brain. Prolactin is behind the feeling of letdown after a big goal has been achieved. Celebrate your wins and victories briefly and then shift to working towards the next step.

Managing dopamine in classrooms (a starter kit)

A full discussion of this takes me several hours to present at schools, but let's cover some of the basics.

Teachers can regulate dopamine schedules to optimise engagement, motivation, and learning. This doesn't involve convincing students to be motivated or providing hearty pep talks. Regulating dopamine in classrooms involves creating the optimal conditions for dopamine to rise and fall over a learning time.

Too many of our students come in the morning with sleep deprivation and lowered dopamine due to gaming.

Make your classroom brightly lit in the morning. If it is sunny, that is even better.

First thing in the morning is rarely the best time for a well-being catchup, as some students will be grumpy and incommunicative.

Instead ritualise the start of the learning day with one of two options:

1. If they seem depleted and tired, begin with solo activities for the first 5 to 10 minutes, such as creating a concept map of key ideas from your previous lesson. You may need to show prompts and guide some.
2. If they seem more switched on, begin with activities where everyone is involved and no one gets anything wrong. Providing each student with a dopamine "hit" early sets up the lesson and the day for success.

Quizzes, puzzles, putting ideas into orders of importance, "Guess what this picture is about"-type activities related to the topic of the lesson work well. If they can be funny, that is even better.

Mix up activities, do some brief problem-solving, and then turn to someone and share their ideas. Brief social interaction combined with humour increases dopamine.

You can feel when students' dopamine declines – the energy leaves the room.

Let your students know that you think they are smart and, with the help of one of the best teachers in the known universe (i.e., you!), they are going to get even smarter this year.

Incorporating some physical movements, especially rhythmic movements, into your classes will increase dopamine.

The aim is then to intersperse intermittent dopamine wins across a learning lesson and also across a day. This requires careful curation of students' learning experiences across a learning day with knowledge of the biological rhythms (circadian and ultradian) that regulate dopamine, energy, concentration, and learning.

The school day has a rhythm, with predictable peaks and troughs of energy, learning, and dopamine. School scheduling needs to capitalise on this to maximise learning outcomes, especially for neurodivergent kids, but ultimately for all students.

Guerrilla tactics for increasing motivation

Regulating dopamine in learning requires a mixture of new experiences or knowledge including "wins" or successes. Basically, this is a pattern of *strength-finding, mind-stretching* – and repeat.

When we springboard from areas of strengths, we are much more likely to get engagement and an early success that increases dopamine, sustains motivation, and stretches learning.

Once dopamine has been raised, students need to see the relevance of a task and to believe that they can succeed at that task. Without relevance or a good probability of success, they aren't going to attempt the task.

How parents can help

Parents can complete the analysis of learning strengths at www.mylearningstrengths.com either with their child or on their behalf and use the free letter to start a conversation about building on their identified strengths. They can then discuss these with their child's teacher (i.e., you). A full report is also available outlining strategies, strengths, and possible future career areas.

Learning strengths can help neurodivergent kids and their parents understand how to kick-start motivation. Building from a learning strength area that a young person already feels confident in will increase dopamine and help to overcome their worries and fears. Starting with what is easiest builds momentum and motivation.

Success in life is about doing more of what you are good at and less of the things you are not good at. We learn more from our successes than from our failures.

Serena Williams is not well known because she can do mathematics. Einstein wasn't well known because he played football. When you focus on the things you find more enjoyable and interesting, even the things you find harder become easier.

There are three main ways of overcoming procrastination:

1. Start with something small and build momentum.
2. Wait for your dopamine to replenish and try again.
3. Do something you hate even more than the thing you are supposed to be doing.

Let's integrate approaches 1 and 2 to build motivation by linking them to existing learning strengths.

Spatial reasoning

Many kids prefer learning through visuals. Presenting information visually increases understanding and retention of ideas. Many neurodivergent kids are creative thinkers who can develop images and designs with great accuracy and intricacy. Use this to create both a kick-starter as well as something that calms and relaxes them.

Even starting by scribbling on a piece of paper or drawing in the air with your fingertips is a beginning. Laying out different shapes or objects in a sequence or pattern can also build this learning strength.

This can range from simple doodling to the types of activities outlined in Betty Edwards' book, *Drawing on the Right Side of the Brain*.

Perceptual–motor skills

Many neurodivergent kids have sensory sensitivities. Once we know their preferences (sensory seeking, sensory avoiding, or sensory distracting) we can tailor experiences that will engage and motivate them. Parents usually know already what calms and motivates their child.

Pairing learning with physical movements can build this learning strength and also increases muscle memory.

Dancing, swaying, stillness, stomping, pointing, and body twisting are worth considering. Dopamine is enhanced by rhythmic movements. For some, having specific textures or aromas is also helpful in creating focus.

We can build upon existing learning strengths in perceptual–motor skills by asking young people to construct models of key concepts they are learning. We can also ask them to use mathematics to calculate where a thrown ball, paper plane, or javelin will land and then test their theories out.

Concentration and memory

This is a great learning strength to have but it can also limit success. Some neurodivergent kids use their considerable learning strengths in concentration and memory to succeed well at school. However, if we rely just on our memory to succeed, we can neglect to develop the thinking skills that set us up for success at higher levels. Consider extending thinking and logic as another learning strength.

Other kids essentially live "clock-free" lifestyles. Some muck around in school and then wonder why they have to do so much work outside of school. Consider having them sit towards the front in class. If they can focus and listen well while at school, they can save endless hours. This is valuable time that can be used for having fun.

Fun challenges can be a useful way of increasing dopamine and motivation. Memory can be increased by making visual, as well as verbal, explanations of ideas, recalling patterns, trails, and sequences or creating maps from memory.

Planning and sequencing

Neurodivergent kids with strengths in planning and sequencing often like to see their progress towards a goal.

The student could make a detailed plan for learning and put the tasks to be completed into order.

They could use Post-it notes to organise the steps towards a successful outcome. On the first Post-it note they write the successful outcome they have in mind. Then they write the step before that and the step before that. Then they write the first step they could take.

If the student is in the senior years of school, try to limit or disable social media pages as exams approach. If low motivation has caused the student to fall behind in any subject, organise a working bee to catch up. Ask others to help. Students can ask teachers to help by saying something like: "I lost motivation for a while in this subject but now I'd really like to catch up."

If the student has not been in the practice of making notes, they should start. If they feel embarrassed about asking questions in class, they could set a goal of asking one question per class. If that is too embarrassing, they could ask the teacher after class.

Smart people don't know all of the answers. Smart people are clever enough to ask lots of questions.

If they've missed notes, they should ask for copies of them. Then they could write a revision summary for each subject, topic by topic. They could use sticky notes, counters, markers, or objects to sequence the stages or steps in solving a problem or catching up in an area of learning.

If the study area has become a mess, clean it up.

Thinking and logic

Some neurodivergent kids with learning strengths in thinking and logic lose motivation and then incorrectly conclude that school is not a place where they can succeed. Usually this is fear of failure being expressed as avoidance rather than a real life choice. Nevertheless, evaluating the pros and cons of learning and of remaining at school with them is a helpful first step.

Once they have realised that the prospect of 9-to-5 drudgery is not paradise on earth and the probability of becoming a world-famous gamer is, sadly, quite slim, they can begin the process of renewing their enthusiasm for learning.

The idea that "Wherever you go, you show up" can be useful. Motivation is not just something you gain or lose; it is the way you approach your life.

We can all be experts in the art of the excuse.

Kids who have felt unmotivated may have done anything they could think of to avoid studying. The world is full of excuses that you can make: "The dog needs a walk." "I have to finish this computer game and then I'll study." "I'll have a nap and study when I wake up."

We have to be tough enough to do the work BEFORE we do the computer games/TV watching/chat room messaging, etc.

Some will be avidly excited about some areas of learning but dismissive of other areas.

Also, we need to be honest enough to admit that lying in bed, with the computer on, listening to music, with YouTube in the background and Messenger open to chat with friends, is not and will never be studying. Students should have some study time sitting up at a desk or table with NO electronic distractions on.

Students who have been finding motivation elusive should change their usual patterns. For example, they could study in a local library rather than at home or change the room they study in.

Just as you learn to surf best by surfing, you learn to succeed in exams and essays by giving your undivided attention to your study. Students should practise in the same conditions they intend to perform in. While special exam provisions can be made for neurodivergent young people, generally there won't be electronics and music in the exam room.

People smarts

This is one of the most important learning strengths in life, especially for neurodivergent kids. Many of them may miss other people's emotional tones and expressions but are able to become skilled readers of their behaviours and what these might indicate about their inner feelings. This skill is valuable in friendship, in workplaces, and eventually in romantic relationships.

People have who not developed a strength in this learning area can progress rapidly. One method is to watch video or film clips with the sound down and try to guess what's going on. Then watch them again with the sound on. Over time, astuteness in reading people will improve.

Other useful techniques are:

- Use pictures of faces to develop emotional detection skills.
- Discuss different types of communication, including texting, talking, emotional signalling, posture, and body language.
- Watch how people move. What emotions do different movements convey?

For kids who are already strong in this area, thinking about the people who will be impressed when they succeed increases dopamine.

Language and word smarts

Many kids find stories enchanting. Creating stories about the key pieces of information they need to learn assists their motivation.

If they have been dopamine depleted, some will be initially reluctant to create or express stories. Suggesting a series of inviting opening lines and then devising a story alternating lines generated by yourself and by them can overcome this.

Use graphic and audio novels or podcasts to re-engage these kids in discussions around ideas.

Help them to learn that words are to authors as paints are to artists. You can create images through words. Ask them to write a vivid account so the reader can almost "feel" the sensation of peeling an orange or escaping from a monster.

Number smarts

Even kids with learning strengths in this area can find expressing or explaining concepts to be stressful. Stress unduly impairs the language circuits in our brain.

Rather than starting with verbal explanations, ask kids to illustrate number problems. They could picture number problems as pie charts, pizza slices, flowcharts, or percentages of people.

Where possible, use movement-based, physical, real-world mathematics activities, such as measuring an area and mapping.

For students who are yet to develop learning strengths in numbers, use whichever area they are already strong in and relate it to numbers.

Chapter 5

Gang leadership and guerrilla dynamics for teachers

As a teacher, you are in the business of running a gang. If you don't run your gang, someone else will run it for you – and you may not like that. So, let's get into the interesting business of gang leadership for teachers.

Life cycle of classrooms

In 1965, Bruce Tuckman outlined the five stages of team and group dynamics as:

1. Forming
2. Storming
3. Norming
4. Performing
5. Ending or adjourning.

This applies to classrooms, sports teams, work teams, and also to whole school cultures.

While we would all like our students to be at the performing stage as quickly as possible, it seems that these different phases are necessary for the development of an effective class and occur at fairly predictable times of the year.

As mentioned earlier, my research indicates a need for people in resilient schools to *connect*, *protect* and *respect* one another. These behaviours fit with Tuckman's life cycle of teams and classrooms:

- **Connect** – forming
- **Protect** – storming and norming
- **Respect** – performing and ending.

1 The forming stage

Early in the year, students are looking to you for guidance. Can I make friends here? Will you like me? Can I trust you? Can I trust me? Can I be successful?

It is a mixture of excitement and apprehension.

Time spent on building positive relationships now will be rewarded with greater performance later. Have every student feel valued. What is appreciated, appreciates.

Break the seal early

Build a culture of co-operation. In the first few days aim to have everyone speak, ask at least one question, and contribute to or extend an idea. Students who appear evasive need you to connect with them personally before they will open themselves to the class.

Ask individual students for help with minor tasks (moving a chair, handing out some notes). If they decline your kind request, ask someone else, BUT come back to them later and make further requests (and keep on making them). The message you want to gently model is that *everyone* contributes in your class.

Get parents onside early

Having students' parents as allies is a significant advantage. Ask them to access www.mylearningstrengths.com to analyse their child's learning strengths.

Ask parents to let you know how their child learns best and what their child is like at their very best.

Succeed early, succeed often

Use everyone's name at least once in the first few days. Give every student a sense of success.

Success is contagious. Go on a treasure hunt with your students. Find their skills, abilities, interests, passions, and learning strengths. Highlight these. If they seem bashful or shy about their own inner gold, do it quietly and privately, but make sure they know that you know they can be great. This is not the year to be half-hearted about getting smarter and being successful.

Mix them up

Use different groupings of students early on. Mix them up. Have your students up and moving and sharing ideas with one another from your first class with them, and then keep doing this throughout the year. For example: "Stand up please. You have three minutes to find out three different ideas from three different people. Go!"

Tell them, "You are all smart, but none of us is as smart as all of us. Go and find out what others think."

What you will see during the forming stage

Students may need a lot of reassurance and may ask lots of questions at this time. Their reliance on you reflects their trust in you and the depth of your relationship. Be proud if they feel overly reliant on you early, as we can make them more self-reliant later on.

Behaviours observed during the forming stage may include lots of questions from students reflecting both their excitement about the new year and the uncertainty or anxiety they might be feeling about their place socially and academically in the group.

What you will feel during the forming stage

As they are so reliant on you for guidance, you may feel they are overly dependent on you. Be patient. Feeling like you are the centre of attention is a sign of success during this stage.

Some students will be anxious. Some will start out being overly reliant, while others will appear detached and distant. Find a way to keep in connection with each student as an individual.

Learn something about each of them (Stuart has a dog named Ruff, Ali's aunt is an actress, Alba loves soccer, etc.).

Gradually increase the amount of independent work that they do.

What your priorities are during the forming stage

Your priorities are to create shared experiences where all of your students get to know one another and can develop ways of collectively learning and solving problems.

People bond when they do things together. Ideas and contributions are valued and treated respectfully by the teacher. For example, the class might be working on a history of inventions or a history of ideas. Different groups might work on specific time periods, with collaboration being encouraged. The collective presentation for each of the groups should amount to more than the sum of its parts. Celebrate their collective success.

At this stage students' sense of belonging to your class is more important than their sense of connection to their house, year level, or school.

Model the way you want your students to act. Follow through on your word. If you can't, apologise and explain why. Be polite and respectful at all times.

Activities that are useful during the forming stage

- Greet all of your students as they come in.
- Ask each student to help you in some small way early on.
- Organise treasure hunts (to highlight interests).
- Create class résumés (all of the sports, games, skills, and interests of the entire class).
- Discuss interesting concepts or ethical dilemmas where there is no one answer (which supports building the idea of multiple perspectives and contributions).

By the end of the forming stage, students think of themselves as valued members of the class.

How you will know the forming stage is finishing

The shift from forming to storming can be a bit of a shock if you are not prepared for it. Students who seemed engaged suddenly jostle with one another. Frictions appear. This is the class recognising individual differences. It can feel like hell, but it is actually growth.

In the forming stage, students look to the teacher for guidance, support, and direction. In the storming stage, they become more focused on themselves and each other. Hold on to your hat and take a deep breath.

2 The storming stage

Just when it was all going so well, the class shifts from forming to storming. There is a whiff of rebellion and insurrection in the air accompanied by the rumblings of discontent.

It is not you. It really is them!

Teachers often worry that they have caused this decline. While storming rarely feels great, it is the group growing in the sense of acknowledging differences between one another.

When you helped the class to form, students gained an early but fragile sense of group identity. Now, as they share their contributions, a clash of experiences and preferences occurs. They are not as similar as they initially thought.

The focus of students moves away from looking to you, their teacher, for guidance, towards comparing and jostling with one another. Students may be less polite, and frustrations or disagreements are more vehemently expressed.

Students scrap with one another. Disputes of the "he said/she said" and "it's not fair" variety break out.

No conflict, no growth

If you are a teacher, it is likely that you chose your profession to help people. This usually means that you do not like conflict (me too!).

As a result, difficult conversations are hard for you (me too, again!), and you are not trained to deal with conflict. This may not be the case for some of your students who sadly have been handling conflict all their lives. Some of them are seasoned professionals in this area.

In most areas of life, conflict arises when there is a clash of different agendas. Conflict is often like a debating competition – one person wants things to change; the other wants things to stay the same. This debate needs to occur for people to develop. It is not that there is debate, it is how the debate is conducted that matters.

Teachers who are prepared for storming and have worked through class behavioural principles in advance can find growth at this time. Teachers who arrive at the storming stage unprepared often get stuck, take it personally, and struggle.

We want to get our students past this stage and into norming as quickly as possible. That is why understanding this stage and having some strategies is so important.

Classrooms that get stuck in storming are terrible places to learn, with unresolved blame and shame. Students stuck in storming either act out or zone out. Teachers stuck in storming feel hurt and become disillusioned and unfairly question their competence.

Social safety rules

You may want to keep progressing the curriculum while the class seems preoccupied with inter-personal issues. However, teaching on regardless is not going to cut it. Until the class resolves these issues, they won't feel safe enough to give you their full concentration.

Don't over-personalise this

It is easy to think this is disrespect and disruptiveness that needs to be squashed, but if you come down too hard on stopping disagreements, you can stifle their development. It is helpful to adopt the position that students are welcome to disagree but are required to do so politely and reasonably respectfully. You need to try to steer the class towards a respectful appreciation of differences in each other.

Personalise and differentiate success

Being successful does not mean someone else has to fail. If a hierarchy is allowed to flourish at this stage, the class will divide into a small number of students who will succeed and dominate and a larger group who will become disengaged and resentful. Find ways of ensuring that each student has some success in their own right.

Strengthen your individual relationships with each student during the storming stage. Be aware of who has not spoken or has avoided eye contact with you and make it your mission to connect with them. They might be able to duck and weave, but don't let them hide.

CARE coaching

A model for helpful conversations is:

- **C** Connect
- **A** Ask and access strengths
- **R** Reassure
- **E** Empower and/or enact.

What you will feel during the storming stage

The honeymoon is over. Pecking orders and hierarchies dominate. You will feel nostalgic for the hazy early days of the year. You'll wonder if you have "lost your touch". You may be tempted to double down and work really hard on developing a project that you hope will really grab their interest.

You can't entertain students out of storming. Until they feel safe to learn in one another's company, the most exciting project on the planet will not sustain their interest.

What you will see during the storming stage

Snitchy, tetchy, and grumpy behaviours are never a lot of fun. Frustration or disagreements that should be minor quibbles boil over and erupt into something much larger than is warranted.

During the storming stage, students may argue or become critical of their classmates or the teacher. Some may even co-opt their parent to express concern.

What your priorities are during the storming stage

Hold your ground. Hold to your values. This is not about "downing tools" until the differences are settled. You are not going to run a group therapy session. You need to find ways for the class to progress without clashing too directly with one another.

As hard as it is, maintain your own kindness and dignity. Model the behaviours you want to see. Refuse to lower your standards.

This big risk in the storming stage is to begin to see the class as a bickering mob. Individualise.

Map the class

Who can you influence directly? Find ways to interact with these students individually. Make small requests of them but don't enforce this if they decline. Indicate that you value them.

Who is going to be influenced by other students? Look at the groupings and seating arrangements. Consider ways to gain some leverage with another influential student.

Who seems out of sorts and beyond any constructive influence at this time? Be prepared to use consequences, but always indicate that "I know you are a better person (or smarter) than this". As best you can, consolidate a relationship with these students that you can build on once this stage has passed.

Activities that are useful during the storming stage

Differentiate tasks as much as you can. Break down learning goals into mini projects. Be selective about the groups of students who can take on a specific project. Allocate roles in each project based on a skill, capacity, or learning strength identified in each student.

If the class spends time with specialist teachers, let them know the groupings and request that specific combinations of students be avoided in their classes too.

If you can, ask the parents of students to complete the analysis at www.mylearningstrengths.com and discuss with you ways you can both build that learning strength in their child or teen.

Be consistent. If you haven't done so already, consider your negotiable and non-negotiable behaviours. Seek support of your colleagues and leadership team over the non-negotiables.

Play fair. Some students will justify their own shoddy behaviour on the basis of "You don't like me". Acknowledge that you may not like some of the ways they are currently going about things, but that you believe in them and know that they can be a great person.

After grouping students into allocated roles in small project teams (usually four or five in each), keep them as busy as you can.

Your aim is to show them how to contribute without competition. Ask them to present ideas and provide constructive suggestions. Check on their progress. If a group is not working, either reallocate roles or restructure the groups.

Essentially you are teaching your class how to collaborate with others.

Of course, not all students will suddenly re-enthuse themselves about learning and become considerate model citizens of a civilised society. Be the time lord. Follow up negative behaviours at a time and place of your choosing, one on one, ideally after class.

Be direct. For example: "I am not happy about the way you behaved in my class today. I am not going to allow you to treat others that way, partly because I wouldn't let other people treat *you* that way in my class. Now you have a choice: I can either impose a consequence or you can promise me that you are going to behave differently in future."

Some may look perplexed. Outline how you *do* want them to act and treat others. Then repeat the statement: "I can either impose a consequence or you can promise me that you are going to behave differently in future. What is your decision?" Take them at their word but quietly reserve the right to impose a consequence if they don't change their ways.

Others may feign indifference and give the impression that you are over-reacting. Be firm and clear. Consider saying, "Even if this doesn't matter to you, that doesn't mean it doesn't matter to someone else." Then repeat your request for their decision.

How you will know the storming stage is finishing

Storming often feels endless, but the tide will turn. We can all feel less than competent during this stage. It is tough, but it is important not to become punitive. Just because they are having a childhood or teen drama does not mean you should have a drama with them.

School staff need to collaborate themselves if they hope to teach their students how to collaborate.

An important aspect of school is learning how to get along with different people and collaborate with them.

The shift in classroom dynamics is subtle at first. It is almost as if they can't be bothered arguing any more. The energy and heat go out of disputes. Friction seems less. Don't highlight to the class that you have noticed a change (they could revert just to prove you wrong).

Reinforce contributions and encourage different inputs and perspectives. For example: "Interesting idea, Izzy! David, have you got a different way of thinking about this?"

Your aim is to, as seamlessly as possible, shift them to the next stage – norming – when we consolidate the habits and routines of positive contribution and learning.

③ The norming stage

After being distracted by bickering and competing with one another, the class once again looks to the wisest, smartest, and most skilled person in the room (you!) for leadership.

The dust has settled. It is the calm after the storm. It is time for a new beginning. If you can, implement new topics and different approaches to the ones you have used. (It is likely you already have a few ideas from your desperate search for solutions when the class was storming.) It is time for a circuit breaker.

The feeling of the class has shifted. While there are still groupings of special BFFs, there is more cohesion across the class.

This is the time when the class may create their own words and inside jokes. Nicknames emerge (try to find out what yours is). These are badges of acceptance and belonging.

Disagreements will still occur, but now they are less frequent and almost always can be resolved within the class positively.

Here everyone gets smart

Great classes are built on the contribution each person makes. Some will make greater contributions because of circumstance or because of greater knowledge. One student may contribute more because they are more skilled, but every student is valued and respected and no one is belittled.

Use contributions to strengthen belonging and progress learning. For example: "That's a great idea, Emily, thank you. Joshua, can you build on Emily's idea and apply it to …" If Joshua looks blank or shrugs his shoulders, turn to one of Joshua's trusted friends and say, "Harry, what would you suggest Joshua could consider?" If Harry also is empty of ideas, coach him: "Yes, it's a tricky one, Harry. Two ideas I have are … or … Which one would you recommend?"

The spirit of this is that everyone has a valuable contribution to make and will be asked by you to make it. You are also the safety net. You are not going to leave them floundering and looking silly. Be a cheerleader and coach for their success.

During this stage, you are building a culture of co-operation. Students look out for and after each other. They are no longer bystanders and are becoming upstanders.

What you will see during the norming stage

During norming, productivity starts to increase in both individual and collective class work.

Create the setting for more frequent and more varied communication among students. Students who appear to have little in common find themselves in a web of problem-solving conversations that you have woven. Over time, this increases their willingness to share ideas or to ask classmates for help.

Students expect delegated tasks and projects from their teacher. Teachers delegate more. They continue to monitor class progress and processes, staying alert for signs of relapse into storming, and continue to deepen relationships, not through friendship but through shared classroom experiences. Teachers also lobby the school to get the resources the class needs.

Students take on responsibilities and are actively pursuing classroom goals. Things mostly run smoothly.

What you will feel during the norming stage

Your initial feeling may be of relief. Your friends and family may share this feeling as you become less fixated on discussing work challenges in social settings.

Your feeling of relief may be followed by trying to explain the change as due to a holiday or long weekend rather than a shift in classroom dynamics. However, dismissing the idea that the classroom dynamics have shifted to a new stage runs the risk of you missing an opportunity.

Your leadership of the class during norming will set your students up for the rest of the year. Their exploration of ideas will be in direct proportion to their assessment of the safety of speaking up and sharing ideas. The safer they feel, the more they will learn.

Your facilitation of their interactions and communications is essential.

You will be active. Steer the class towards cohesive learning – seeking a suggestion from a student who is drifting into a daydream there, while smiling at a student who needs acknowledgement as you ask a challenging question to a table of students at the back, while standing by the side of another student who needs your presence to settle themselves.

Move around the class. You are demonstrating how to participate and make a contribution.

What your priorities are during the norming stage

The role of a teacher during the norming stage is like a conductor leading different elements of an orchestra to experience success.

A key challenge in this stage is to keep students motivated and engaged. Tell them they are the best class you have ever taught.

You will gain power and influence by handing over power and influence. Delegation, small groupwork, and power sharing are indicative of an effective teaching style. By trusting your students, they will begin to trust you and will eventually broaden their trust to most of the class. Teaching is more relational.

Re-engage parents. If there are any residual concerns lingering from the storming stage, try to resolve these. It is time to move ahead and plan how to capitalise on each student's learning strengths to have a great outcome this year. Together with each parent, plan how to promote a specific learning strength in their child.

Students feel attached to the class as something "greater than the sum of its parts" and feel some pride in being a member of the class. Students feel confident in their own abilities and those of their classmates. They begin to rely on one another.

Delegate responsibility to your students as much as you can. Students become involved in decision-making and conflict resolution as well as researching new learning opportunities.

Roles and responsibilities are clear and accepted. Big decisions are made by group agreement. Smaller decisions may be delegated to individuals or small teams within the group.

The class is able to work towards achieving the goal and also to attend to relationship, style, and process issues along the way. Students care for one another.

Activities that are useful during the norming stage

Challenges build dopamine (the neurochemical of motivation). Group challenges strengthen group identity.

Start most classes with an intriguing puzzle: what's going on in this picture, illusions, odd questions that initially stump the class, 20 questions, what happened on a specific date in history, or what is the similarity between two seemingly unrelated events.

Having the class feel collectively bewildered at times is useful. Challenges and shared activities bond people. They also help you to teach your students that they are capable, can do research, and can figure things out: "Ok, so no one knows, AND my class are much smarter than they know, SO how can we go about finding out?"

Oxytocin is the neurochemical and hormone of belonging and trust. When we complete activities together, we deepen our sense of connection and mutual trust. This is why some people develop deep friendships with some of their work colleagues.

In your classroom, you want a mixture of whole group activities and selected smaller group activities. This increases group cohesion as well as bonding between smaller groups of students.

Collaborative learning or small group work is a powerful way of accelerating student learning. You could base groups on interests, learning strengths, skills, or physical attributes such as height. Mix them up over time. Don't allow groupings to coagulate.

The GET IT! model of learning indicates that specific times of a lesson are better for whole group or small group activities:

- **G** **Getting ready to learn** – whole class sometimes followed by pairings
- **E** **Experiencing difference** – whole group
- **T** **Trying it out** – small groups
- **I** **Information processing** – whole group sometimes with smaller group investigations
- **T** **Transfer of learning** – small groups lead to whole group discussion at the end of the lesson.

How you will know the norming stage is finishing

The business of the day becomes familiar. You have a reasonable expectation that students will know this is how we do things in your (and eventually our) classroom.

Norming is completed when the class is clear about the expectations and has resolved most of the big conflicts it has faced.

In the performing stage, the class makes significant progress. The orchestra that you have conducted starts to co-ordinate and perform at even higher levels. The time of the year with the most learning gain is about to begin.

4. The performing stage

If only we could have started here, it would have been all so simple. The problem is that no one starts out performing at peak level. It takes time. Groups have to form, storm, and norm before they can perform at their highest level.

There is an odd paradox: we are about six months through the school year and the class is ready to perform well. At around the same time, motivation slumps and weariness peaks.

Increasing dopamine to raise motivation will be critical to get the best out of this stage. Teaching in bursts with intervening rest periods builds dopamine and motivation.

It's time to bring in the heavy lifting – these are the strategies that really create success. Let's surge our level of learning gain.

Every time we improve teaching, learning improves. Teacher-led instruction is the most effective way of improving student outcomes.

What you will see during the performing stage

The bickering and jostling for position are over and the teacher is able to delegate and rely on students. The class performs at a higher level.

A "can do" attitude is visible, as are offers to assist one another. Roles may have become more fluid, with students taking on various roles and responsibilities as needed. Differences among members are appreciated and used to enhance the class's performance.

In the performing stage the class makes significant progress. Commitment to learning is high, and the competence of students also increases. Students should continue to deepen their knowledge and skills, including working to continuously improve learning outcomes. Accomplishments in class process or progress are measured and celebrated.

A resilient mindset is visible, as are offers from students to assist one another.

What you will feel during the performing stage

You may feel surprised, and it could take you a few days before you become aware that the class is humming along.

During the performing stage, students feel satisfaction in the class's progress. They share insights about process and are more aware of their own (and each other's) strengths and limitations. Students feel attached to the class as something "greater than the sum of its parts" and feel satisfaction in being part of the class. Students' confidence in their individual abilities and those of their classmates grows.

What your priorities are during the performing stage

- Delegating roles and tasks
- Valuing every student's different contribution
- Looking at problems and conflicts as learning opportunities
- Finding time for fun and rest.

Activities that are useful during the performing stage

Here are key strategies for teaching effectively to increase student learning:

- **Removing unnecessary noise.** Try to implement "just take a minute". This is a minute of silence to consider an idea or review notes or think before answering.
- **Identifying similarities and differences.** This builds abstract thought and increases memory.
- **Summarising and taking notes.** Picking out the most important ideas and organising information deepens thinking.

- **Reinforcing effort and providing recognition.** Let your students know you think they are smart and at this stage of the year are about to get even smarter. Involve their parents in an analysis of learning strengths at www.mylearningstrengths.com.
- **Doing research (homework and practice).** Teach students how to work smarter, not harder, by doing 20-minute sprints of research.
- **Introducing the idea of deliberate practice.** This is where students take part in structured and purposeful behaviours under the guidance of a teacher to advance their learning.
- **Presenting information non-verbally.** Use rubrics to encourage students to present ideas in a variety of ways through movement, pictures, video, or poster creation. Consider asking students to produce a one-page summary that is visually interesting on a key concept.
- **Try co-operative learning.** Even if you felt that small group work was too precarious earlier in the year, it is time to give this another trial. Expect a few teething issues as students move from pair-share to small group (four is often best) activities.
- **Setting objectives and providing feedback.** The smaller the target the easier it is to hit it. Set small goals and then support them in surpassing them. Give them positive feedback and outline next steps.
- **Generating and testing hypotheses.** Apply the scientific method to thinking – information gathering, forming hypotheses, testing ideas, and re-forming theories. Find odd or quirky aspects of the topics you are teaching or ethical issues and let the class wrestle with ideas and solutions.
- **Using cues, questions and advance organisers.** Socratic questioning deepens reflective thinking. Provide students with

a road map of what you are going to accomplish between now and the end of the school year.
- **Build and maintain positive relationships.** Always be your students' biggest advocate and supporter. Believe in them and be on their side as much as you can. Find ways to Connect with, Protect, and Respect your students.
- **Metacognition and meta-learning.** Metacognition and meta-learning involve knowing how our brain learns best and being able to think about how we think. Knowing this helps us to leverage our own strengths. This sets everyone up for success in life. This self-awareness directly increases self-efficacy.

How you will know the performing stage is finishing

Just as we often sense the seasons are shifting before the date the new season is due to commence, there are small signs that tell us the group is shifting.

As this time of the year is often hectic for teachers, it is easy to overlook these signs.

While the class is still productive, you will need to intersperse new learning with more activities and revision of key ideas.

To keep motivation and dopamine well-regulated, you will need to use more quizzes, puzzles, social interaction, small group work, and humour.

In the staff room, the focus of discussion is often on how much teachers need to get done by the end of the year. Calmly take this on and know that careful planning now pays off.

Students and parents are gearing up for final assessments, so anxiety can increase. Be methodical and prepare students well.

Younger students and their families shift their focus towards wrapping up the year and forthcoming holidays. There can be a mismatch between teachers' desire to have everything completed and reported on and students wanting to wind down. This is why the next stage – ending – is so important to do well.

The ending stage

We often don't mark the ending or the completion of our important relationships well.

This can rob us of the rituals that signify to us that we are leaving one way of being and entering another. Acknowledging that we are passing through a threshold helps us all to develop and grow. The challenges and opportunities of the next year will be different from those faced this year.

While it is good to have celebratory rituals, we also need to take time to reflect on how the past year has changed us, what we have learned, and how we can use this year to develop even further next year.

If we rush this time of year, we risk insufficiently acknowledging the importance of the people we have shared time and experiences with. Endings are just as important as beginnings.

Ending well

Ending involves the breakup of the class at the end of the year. Students can move on to new things, feeling good about what's been achieved. You can move towards a well-earned break.

Recognition of and sensitivity to students' vulnerabilities is helpful, particularly if students have been closely bonded to you or to one another and feel a sense of insecurity or threat from this change.

Students may feel a mix of sadness or a sense of loss about the changes coming to their class as well as pleasure in their achievements. Given these conflicting feelings, class morale may rise or fall throughout the ending stage.

While ending, some class members may become more sensitive and less focused on tasks, and their productivity may drop.

Effective ending assists students to take away the best of their experiences to apply in the future.

What you will see during the ending stage

During the ending stage, the energy and focus of some students may drop.

It is important to remember that for some of your students their only experience of relationships ending has been dramatic and disastrous.

Other students may find focusing on learning at hand is an effective response to their sadness or sense of loss. Their productivity may increase.

What you will feel during the ending stage

It is a mixed time of the year. You may feel exhausted, run off your feet, pleased with what has been achieved, excited about having a break, and sad about losing a connection with your students, all at the same time.

Make sure you get enough sleep. There is little point frantically rushing to the last day of the school year and then collapsing in an exhausted heap and being sick for most of your holidays.

At the start of each term, try to plan to have the end of term mentally end in the middle of the last week, so you and your students have two days to unwind before the break.

Students may feel a variety of concerns about the class's impending dissolution. They may be feeling some anxiety because of uncertainty about their individual role or future friendships.

They may feel sadness or a sense of loss about the changes coming to their relationships. At the same time, students may feel a sense of satisfaction with their own accomplishments.

It is highly likely that at any given moment students will be experiencing different emotions about the class's ending.

What your priorities are during the ending stage

The end of the year creates a natural review point for everyone. While any year is a mix of highs and lows, encapsulating the past year into a dominant narrative can be helpful.

Some useful questions and discussion points might be:

- "When you look back on this year, what would you say was the hardest time?" (Often students find it easiest to express their most negative experiences first.)
- "I'm sorry that happened, did it change?"
- "If it hasn't changed, what have you learned from this year about what not to have in your future?"
- "If it has changed, how did you change it? What did you do first? What worked best?"
- "What worked best for you this year? Was there a highlight or a best moment? How did that come about?"
- "How do you think you could make more of that happen next year?"
- "What did you learn about yourself this year?"
- "What parts of yourself changed?" (You might wish to highlight a positive change you have noticed in each of your students.)

It might then be useful to do a complete review of the year from your perspective, highlighting particular contributions or moments month by month (ensure you mention every student in your class!).

The class needs to acknowledge the upcoming transition and the variety of ways that each student and the entire class may be feeling about the class's impending dissolution.

During this stage, the class should focus on three tasks:

1. Ending well by completing any final work
2. Evaluating the class's process, with a particular focus on identifying "lessons learned"
3. Creating a closing celebration that acknowledges the contributions of individuals and the accomplishments of the class.

Effective ending assists students to take away the best of their experiences to apply in the future.

Connect	Protect	Respect
Forming		
Connect with each student individually, building relationships and a sense of belonging. Connect with what they have that is their own contribution to make.	Protect their self-efficacy and self-belief. Some students have a history of despair about their abilities and lose motivation. Be the antidote by protecting their hope that they can succeed.	Respect that they will develop from this stage of the year to grow into a more mature form of themselves. Interact with them in a way that indicates they have infinite potential.
Storming		
Know that storming feels hard but is a sign of growth. While thinking about group processes, preserve your individual relationships with students.	Protect their sense that they have a contribution to make that is unique to them. Differences are to be called upon and celebrated.	Respect that they have to resolve peer issues in order to feel safe enough to learn. Respect that your own sense of kindness will eventually prevail.

Connect	Protect	Respect
Norming		
Implement routines, protocols, and rhythms of the day that create a sense of dependability and security.	Guard students who appear to be anxious or avoidant and help them to develop a resilient mindset. Calm the agitated and directly link with the avoidants.	Respect that they will need short bursts of fun, movement, and social interaction interspersed into learning times to maintain levels of belonging and enthusiasm. Keep energy levels high.
Performing		
Connect with students as they learn best, focusing on their learning strengths and their interests.	Don't just cover content; develop skills. Deepen their ability to research, think about, and discuss ideas. Develop problem-solving skills and creative thinking.	Respect the practices you instil at the stage where you set them up as successful learners for life.
Ending		
Connect with the best of what has happened throughout the year.	Protect their successes and accomplishments. We miss a golden opportunity if we can't take the best of our achievements from the past year into the next.	They often have unexpressed apprehension about the next year. Reassure them that this year sets them up well for next year. Respect yourself for all that you have done this year.

Chapter 6
Wheeling and dealing

You don't have to be shifty to succeed as a teacher, but a bit of basic rat-like cunning won't go astray.

Most schools have an immune system that rejects or delays new or revolutionary ideas. Watch carefully how this is done in staff meetings. In your first few months at any school, it is always wise to try to learn how this operates and to be aware of the process. The questions to ask yourself are: "How are new ideas kept from changing things? Who speaks and who is silent? Which issues are ignored or sidelined?"

Learning this will help you to understand that it is pointless to become embroiled in futile missions to change the school and will help you later on when you really do want something to change.

Meetings

Some schools have more meetings and committees than some of the largest corporations I work with. Meetings can drain vital life energy away from you with mind-numbing ease or can eat into your precious non-work time. Of course, some meetings are important. Try to select carefully.

Go to as few meetings as you possibly can get away with. If you are just starting at a school, not attending a meeting that you didn't realise you were supposed to attend is a lot better than going to a meeting you didn't need to attend and ending up lumbered with additional responsibilities.

Quietly, find out which meetings are essential to go to. You may not be able to control many meetings, but try to reduce meetings and meeting times. Decline to go to some. Consider politely leaving meetings when your bit is finished. Gently ask about the agenda for the meeting. If you have to convene a meeting, have standing up or walking meetings. Get some exercise while you walk around the school discussing whatever you need to discuss.

As Richard Harkness once commented, "What is a committee? A group of the unwilling, picked from the unfit, to do the unnecessary". If you refer back to the earlier chart on the relationship between group size and group IQ (see page 32), you'll see why large committees rarely work.

At one stage of my life, I worked in a job that involved some of the most mind-numbing, brain-withering meetings known to humankind. A few colleagues and myself decided to liven meetings up by having a secret competition. Before each meeting, we would select an unusual word. "Turmeric" and "asparagus" are two that particularly remain in my memory. The competition winner was the first person who used the word in a logical way during the meeting. Some examples:

> The consultant is as rich as the colour of turmeric.
> This plan has all the power of a piece of cooked asparagus.

The majority of meeting participants who weren't in on the competition must have been mystified why meetings would suddenly abound with references to turmeric or asparagus, but it sure made them a lot of fun for us.

Requests for additional work

Some bosses will come to you saying, "Here's something I'd like you to do. I'm not exactly sure what I want, but I'm sure you'll figure it out, and we have no additional resources to achieve it."

Schools are vulnerable to the whims and fads of councils or boards, education departments, the media, and the odd student petition. The problem is: just as quickly as these urgent needs arise, they tend to fade away (all too often only to be replaced by the next wave of fads). If you are the bunny trying to deal with whatever was so life-threateningly urgent last week, you can end up spending a lot of time doing work that matters to no one.

Each year there is a professional appraisal system in most schools. Use this to your advantage. Ask your line manager to clearly outline the key priority areas that he or she would like you to address over the next term or year. Write these down. After the meeting, send your line manager a written letter or email outlining the key areas and seeking confirmation that these are exactly what is wanted.

If future requests are made of you that would divert your energies from the priorities outlined in the appraisal meeting, you can respond by saying, "I'd be delighted to help out, and which of the key priority areas should we replace?" Save yourself for that request that you are passionate about and probably would have done anyway. Then do a great job and enjoy doing it.

Resourceful people need resources

Given the haste and stress of school days, it is very handy to have a collection of your own objects and belongings around.

Your shopping and gathering list

Good things to have in or around your desk (label them or lose them!):

Survival items
- Water bottle
- Snacks, such as trail mix
- Aspirin, Berocca tablets (for yourself)
- Cough lozenges
- Map of the school
- Phone numbers of substitute teachers
- Small first aid kit
- Late bus schedules
- Procedures for accessing TV and Internet
- Calendar for the year
- Sanitised wipes (you'll be amazed how many uses you'll find for these little suckers!)
- Antibacterial handwash.

Stationery items
- Post-it notes
- Pens
- Coloured pencils
- Stickers, stamps
- Staplers, staples
- Scissors
- Extra file holders

- Liquid paper
- Calculator
- Paperclips, rubber bands
- Glue sticks
- Pencil sharpeners, hole punchers.

Professional items
- Duty rosters
- Curriculum guides
- Marks book
- All official school forms
- Office memos
- Parent email address and phone list
- List of parent volunteers.

Desirable
- A digital camera (to take photos of students doing things well – if the school permits you to do this – check first)
- A book you are currently reading
- Lunch menus from local eating places
- An audible timer (like those you see in hairdressers)
- An audio player
- Several boxes of thank-you cards to use for colleagues, staff, and parents.

Chapter 7
Time making

What if you could maximise positive gains in your life in less time? Essentially you would be in the business of making time. While everyone around is spending time, you'd be sitting back, doing more with less effort in less time.

If you get a choice in teaching to be either the hare or the tortoise, always choose to be the tortoise.

The Pareto principle indicates that you will get 80% of your impact from 20% of your activities. Let's talk about how to access and use the 20% that creates the maximal impact.

Schools are often busy, sometimes frantic places that can value energy over wisdom. For a sustainable career, however, you need to value wisdom over energy. Sure, I know you are young, vibrant, and good-looking with energy to burn. Even so, find some ways to make time and save energy for your own life and the partying and still do a great job.

Our most precious, irreplaceable resource is our time. If you are very, very lucky, you will get on average 4,000 weeks of it to allocate.

This chapter is filled with a collection of ideas that you could try out to make time.

1 Time making in your life

One year defining activity

Make each year memorable. Try to take on a challenge, adventure, or new interest area or develop a new skill, so that 10 years from now you will be able to look back and say, "Oh, that was the year I went to Japan/learned tap dancing/started to speak Swahili" and so on.

Six mini-adventures

Alongside a major activity for the year, you might also consider setting up for yourself six mini-adventures scattered throughout the year that act as circuit breakers for your life and refresh you.

Put more on your plate of the things you love to do

Giving priority to the things and people we love takes determination. The world is always ready to use up almost every available moment of your life. Determined scheduling is challenging but also important for you to create a life you love.

Visual calendar

Even if you have an electronic diary, also keep a paper diary. Use a week-to-a-page diary so you can gain an overview of the week ahead. This facilitates planning and time allocation.

Stephen Covey, in his wonderful book *First Things First*, recommended a system I have followed for years. Specify seven major roles of your life. The first one is always self-care. For example, you might have self-care, partner, family, friend, netballer, reader, and educator.

At the start of the week (usually on a Sunday evening), go through each of your seven roles and write down one thing you could do in the forthcoming week that would make a positive difference in each area.

This shifts your life from being reactive to being intentional.

To-do and to-don't lists

You may be someone who wants to do more things than you have the time available to do. This requires that you prioritise.

Firstly, create a table with as many rows as you like and write down all the activities you want to do. You can keep adding to this table as new ideas occur to you.

Develop a second priority table with only five rows. These are your top five priority activities. It is only when one of your top five has been accomplished or completed that you can free up a space on this table.

Once a space has been freed up on your priority table, you can then move an activity from your first table to your second.

Time windows

Most of us have predictable times of the day when we get stuff done and other times when we are a bit fog-headed and unproductive. Learn your own pattern and use these times well.

Outsource your weaknesses

In this time of AI we can think more ruthlessly about outsourcing some parts of our work. While there are some areas of your life that you delight in and where your own hands-on creative touch makes a difference, there are also areas that are uninspiring drudgery for you.

Eat the frog first

Mark Twain once said, "If it's your job to eat a frog, it's best to do it first thing in the morning. And if it's your job to eat two frogs, it's best to eat the biggest one first". Your willpower is strongest in the morning, so do the tough stuff first.

Time making in your classroom

Identify the time soakers

For a few weeks note how you spend your time. Identify time soakers. These can be tasks or people who take up a lot of your time. What activities repeat? What soaks up your valuable time?

Checklists

Make checklists for recurring events. Include on the list everything that must be done before, during and after the event, then check off as completed.

Automate and bundle

There are things you will use year after year. Make them as automatic as possible. Block out a time at the beginning of the month or a new unit to take care of all the small things, like changing due dates on assignments you use year after year, all at once.

Manage the paper flood

Get a binder, dividers, a pencil bag, and a hole punch. You'll need to tailor the tabs to suit yourself, but consider the following:

- Memos
- School initiatives
- Marks

- Grading
- Modifications/adjustments
- Student/parent contact information
- Calendar and schedules
- Further reading.

Leave one for lesson plans and reflections.

An A–Z box file is also great for holding odds and ends – file late slips, action plans, and notes under the child's last name. If a concern develops, you have all the paperwork, without having to take a huge amount of time filing.

Some teachers swear by having student files on wheels with two wire drawers below the hanging files. Each student has his/her own file.

Even better, use your computer. Ask other staff how they set up their computer and develop a system that works for you.

Time manage

Priorities! Some people make endless to-do lists and then think they have to tick them all off. A to-do list is not prioritisation. Prioritisation is not just ordering things in terms of importance, it's actually saying: "If I could only do one thing on my to-do list, what would it be?" This becomes your first priority. Then from the remaining list: "If I could only do one thing, what would it be?" That becomes your second priority, and so on.

Keeping students busy

There are always students who finish early while other students need the full period to work. Save the comics from newspapers or puzzles that you find. When students finish early, they can study, help others, read a book they have brought to class, or read the comics or solve the puzzles that you have saved. This keeps the students quiet and engaged while slower students have time to complete their work.

Delegate

Student jobs! The more the kids run the classroom, the more organised, efficient, and smooth it will all be!

At each table, every student should have a job: materials manager (to get up and put materials away), class notebook manager (to collect all of the notebooks around the room), etc.

Original or copy?

Put a broad yellow highlighter mark across the top of the original copy of any material you photocopy. This makes it easy to retrieve and return to your files after use. It sure saves wondering what happened to the original.

Blend the learning

Learning management systems are a good way to employ a blended learning strategy. You introduce topics (via video, tutorials, assignments, and discussion boards) before class, allowing you to dive into greater depth and use your classroom for creative, constructive learning opportunities. Search YouTube and TED-Ed for dozens of videos on blended learning topics, including tutorials, discussions, and real-life examples.

Student reflection

Before handing a piece of work in, students should complete a reflection sheet. This could include:

- I revised this essay at least once.
- I spent at least two hours on this essay.

- I tried to do my best work on this essay.
- I have used the criteria in the rubric.
- I proofread the essay at least twice for grammar and punctuation.
- If I were to revise this paper again, I would …

Marking

Don't mark everything. Excessive marking and endless meetings are activities that suck the souls out of teachers. Time spent on marking is time taken away from planning and preparation for future lessons. You need to have a balance of both, but it is to the detriment of your teaching if marking takes the majority of your time.

Don't multi-task. Focus on one thing at once and finish it. Ask yourself:

- Does it progress a professional goal?
- Is it required today?
- Does it lighten my mental load?

Mark standing up

Teachers regularly report they get through more in less time when they mark at a standing desk.

Do some marking in 1-1 conferences

While the class is completing independent work, call students up to your desk, read their work, and give them marks.

Don't comment on everything

When someone completes work for you, your first two words should always be: "Thank you." The most effective feedback is to point out two things you like and one thing the student could change or improve on. There is a place for in-depth, all-inclusive marking perhaps once a term.

Use dot points

Don't write long sentences when providing feedback. Dot points are more memorable and easier to respond to.

Plan for batch marking

Plan the lessons with heavy marking on days when you have some free time. For example, plan weekly creative writing lessons when you know you have an afternoon of free periods. This allows you to get on top of the marking.

Stickers are great but stamps are quicker

Get a few different stamps made up for different responses.

Winning the email wars

Process emails at scheduled times. Do a quick scan of your inbox to check if there is anything urgent to attend to. Do not open other emails at this time. It's easy to lose focus and very difficult to gain it back.

Turn notifications off. Most importantly, do not check your emails late at night or last thing before going home on a Friday evening.

Your inbox is an assembly line. Your motto from the moment you open your emails should be: read – respond – delete (or archive).

Your own emails should explain who you are, what you want, why you should get it, and when you need it by. If it relates to a date and time, put those in the subject box.

Never, ever use email to give someone negative feedback, share gossip, or make impolite comments about anyone.

Delete

Most of the emails we receive are useless. When you get such an email, just hit the delete button.

Delegate

Some emails are going to trigger an action that needs to be taken, but you might not be the best person for the job. In such cases, all you can do is forward the email to the appropriate person. If you need to follow up to see if the task was completed, put a reminder into your calendar.

Once an email is forwarded, you can either delete it or archive it for future reference.

Respond

Some emails are going to require you to reply to the sender. If you can keep it short and concise (under five sentences), go ahead and reply to the email immediately. If the email requires a longer reply and you currently don't have the time, allocate some time later in the day for in-depth responses.

③ Time-making tips for teachers

1. Always put the agenda on the board for the next day before you leave for home. Even if you are not totally prepared, you look as though you are.
2. Have some routines that are the same every day and that take little effort to put in place. The kids know what to do when they walk into the class.
3. Try to leave everything at school. Try to get assessments done before you leave for home.

4. Do as much field experience as you can BEFORE you get into your own classroom. Observe master teachers. Even observing poor teachers can be a learning experience for you.

5. Laugh with your students and help them enjoy school by showing them that you enjoy being with them. We often get wrapped up in the content delivery and take ourselves (and them) too seriously.

6. Be willing to try anything (anything appropriate anyway) to motivate your students. Don't be afraid of looking stupid. You'd be surprised how doing something off the wall or bizarre can break up the tedium.

7. Take digital pictures of your kids and run them as a screen saver on your classroom computer and as a looping slide show when parents are there. (Some schools require permission to do this, so check first.)

8. Set WFPs – Weekly Family Projects. These are simple, yet fun, projects for the kids to work on with their families each week. You don't need to send them home every week. You don't need to assess them. They can include baby pictures and facts about the student as a baby for the other kids to "guess who", math games, a family timeline – ANYTHING really that can get the families involved in the curriculum (and a great way to complete projects that you might not have time for in school).

9. Always have a back-up lesson ready in case a lesson that you are doing goes over like a wrought-iron hang glider.

10. Always have a stack of extra activities in case your lesson ends early.

Time making

11. Find out when reports are due, and assume that they need to be in the office three weeks beforehand.

12. Get all the shots you need for your job, and consider getting some antiseptic hand wipes. Always wash your hands. Be aware of all the colds and flu's your students will bring with them.

Chapter 8
Curating great learning experiences

When I was young, my uncle, who was a sheep farmer, had a very old and gnarled-looking kelpie dog called "Charlie". Charlie was wise in mysterious ways. While all the other younger dogs would race around the flock of sheep, barking furiously and trying to get them through the gate, Charlie would sit patiently watching. I could almost imagine him leaning back with a cigarette hanging out of the corner of his mouth and a laconic grin on his face. At a time I was never able to precisely determine, Charlie would amble up to the flock and simply lean into the sheep and deftly steer them through the gate. That dog was a master!

Watching Charlie taught me the art of timing.

The science of teaching is more than just techniques. It is not just what you do – it is when and how you do it. Timing is everything. Reading the crowd, sensing their energy, and playing to their strengths are all part of the art and drama of good teaching.

If we synthesise the research findings on how people learn, we can construct a model called GET IT! There are five phases to learning:

- **(G) Getting ready to learn** – focuses on establishing positive attitudes and perceptions, setting objectives, and orienting students to learning.
- **(E) Experiencing difference** – providing accurate new information in a way that builds interest, motivation and intrigue.
- **(T) Trying it out** – experiential, co-operative learning and group work.
- **(I) Information processing** – critical thinking, creative problem solving, creating meaning, identifying similarities and differences, and summarising and note-taking.
- **(T) Transfer** – this is the takeaway message: the transfer of learning to other settings and synthesising and making information stay alive in students' memories.

Using the GET IT! model to design learning experiences

In designing learning experiences, the GET IT! model works in reverse. Planning should occur in the sequence outlined below:

1 Transfer

- What do I want my students to understand?
- What do I want them to apply?
- How can I elicit situations where they could apply it?
- How can I help my students store this information in long-term memory?

- How can I link this information to big questions that have enduring value outside the classroom?

2) Information processing

- What strategies can I use to create and check for understanding and meaning?
- How can I enhance long-term memory storage?
- What summarising, paraphrasing, and note-taking strategies can I use to enhance the processing and retrieval of knowledge?
- How can I help students to develop non-linguistic presentations of the information (metaphors, brain webs, models, analogies, icons)?

3) Trying it out

- What experiential, co-operative learning or group work activities can I devise to give students a chance to use and reflect up the information?
- How can I make using this information fun?

4) Experiencing difference

- How can I intrigue students so that they acquire and integrate knowledge?
- In what ways can I reinforce effort and provide recognition?

5) Getting ready to learn

- How can I create a brain-friendly classroom?
- What can I use to increase dopamine, intrigue, and engagement?
- How can I help a class develop positive attitudes and perceptions towards learning? What rituals may assist in this?
- How can we set objectives and how can I best provide feedback?

How the GET IT! model fits with learning and memory

As you can see from the following diagram, the amount your students retain varies according to where they are in the learning process.

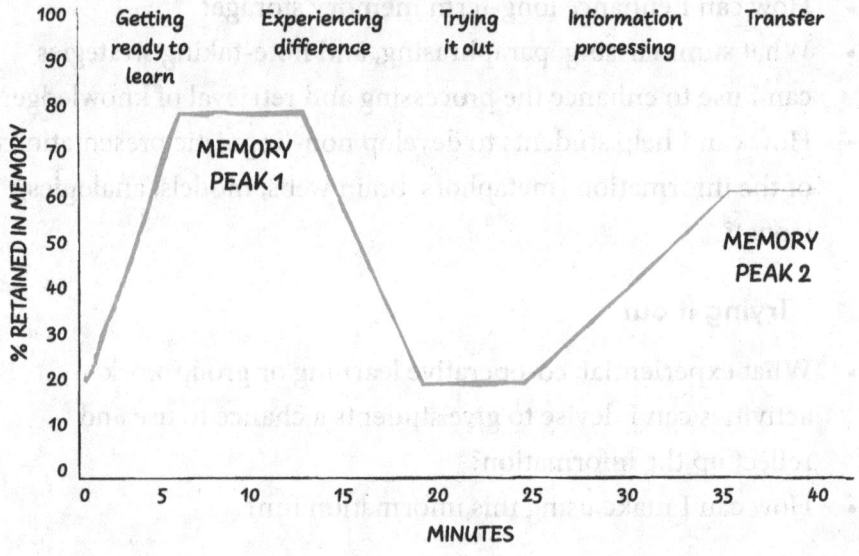

As we saw in Chapter 1, you enter a classroom with all your senses tingling on high alert. Greeting students as you enter, you "read" the room. Who looks weary? Who avoids eye contact? Who is chattering and distracted? Who looks about to slump into a dispirited or comatose state?

Your aim is to convert the restless and the uninterested and inspire the motivated into a class of engaged, knowledgeable learners with a resilient mindset. This work is the "dark arts" of enchantment.

Build social capital as you move around the room. Brief positive greetings and comments count for a lot. Increasing oxytocin deepens a sense of belonging and strengthens trusting relationships.

You curate the learning experience by dividing the lesson into distinct phases while staying on task to achieve your objectives. This goes beyond mindsets to understanding and regulating neurochemistry to enhance learning.

Early on, in the first few minutes it's **Getting ready to learn** time. During this time the objectives of the lesson are established and students are engaged in an active inquiry about the area to be learned.

It is often best to start classes with some visual information. This might include pictures or posters, or you could simply write on the board a message like, "Today's first lesson is about [insert topic area]. Please write down three things you know about this, then go and find your shoe friend and develop a list of eight things you both know about this. You have four minutes."

Alternatively, use routines and quizzes to grab their attention early.

The students will be working and you can keep a close eye on them while you put your feet up and contemplate what you will do after work that day.

Between 5 and 15–20 minutes into the lesson is critical learning time. This is the information that is really going to be remembered. That is why it is a lousy idea to settle kids in class and then do admin or homework checking. It's also not a good idea to use this time to conduct brainstorms that are likely to illicit a series of incorrect responses, because those are the answers they will remember!

This is the **Experiencing difference** time when you use hooks or bewilderment to get students' focus and attention. During this time, try to involve students through activity or intrigue.

This is the time to input new learning so that your students' brains can absorb, analyse, and begin to evaluate information.

Students absorb new information most easily from pictures that are explained by their teacher, especially when key ideas are highlighted (different colours, fonts, or shapes, with students pointing to main ideas).

Our brains love stories. If you can tell a brief story of how this knowledge was discovered, what life was like beforehand, or what we can now do as a result, you will prepare students while increasing intrigue, engagement, and memory. As you do so, develop a visual concept map, adding ideas as you explain them. Ask students to copy the map.

Place key concepts together with the most important ideas in the centre and in close proximity to each other.

This is the time to work hardest in the lesson, because if you can convey new concepts in a way that is relevant or interesting to the students, they will learn it. If you have used the survey in Chapter 1, you will have a good idea of their areas of interest. For example, you might grandly announce that today we are going to learn about the very basis of sex, and then embark on a soap opera description of cellular differentiation to the theme of "Breaking up is hard to do".

No matter how entertaining, dramatic, exciting, or relevant you make the new information, nothing lasts forever. At about 20 minutes into the learning time, the students' eyes will begin to glaze over. It is time to shift your teaching strategy to something more memorable.

Trying it out means giving students a five-minute task to work with others on. Use the flexible groupings outlined earlier. Teaching others, finding out what others know, interviewing others, and demonstration are all good ways to help students to remember new information. This is the "use it or lose it" time of the learning episode, so students should be standing up and talking to a different person than the one they spoke to during the first partner exercise at the start of the class.

Sometimes having music playing softly at this time helps.

When we learn something new, our brain builds a new neural circuit using acetylcholine that is then reinforced with dopamine.

It is time to stand up and form thinking teams. If you know students' learning strengths, use these to form groups (www.mylearningstrengths.com).

The aim is to have students collaborate to reflect on the new knowledge and to create new insights. Keep a display of the concept map or question to be discussed visible.

Our brains store the information for later use. New knowledge is encoded and added to our mental schema. If the information is not reinforced, the brain may simply dismiss it.

Keep students standing and discussing during this time, as this increases blood flow to brains and also builds dopamine and energy.

Select some thinking teams and ask them to share an idea. Then ask students to return to their seats.

If time is too short for thinking teams, having students stand up and turn to a partner can also be effective.

Ending this phase with a one-minute relaxing video, while asking students to be silent and reflect on what they have learned so far, increases memory storage twenty-fold.

Like Charlie, my uncle's sheep dog, this is the time to sniff the breeze. Undoubtedly some groups will work better than others. Stand and hover near those groups that appear a little less functional.

Just a fraction of a second before they go off task is the time to cheerily announce, "Please thank your partners and return to your seat." Turning the music up at this point can also help.

There is often a temptation to chatter after moving around, so it's now time to quickly have students move into **Information processing** mode. This often occurs between the 25 and 35-minute mark of a learning episode.

Information processing can involve some note-taking discussion, evaluation of outcomes, critical thinking, and solving problems. The aim of this phase is deepening understanding and building memory.

Do not overlook the need for students to process the information they have learned in the lesson. Without processing and reflection, knowledge evaporates rapidly.

Learning essentially is a change in long-term memory, and memory is developed through active thinking. This involves creating a new network of links between brain cells. The richer the network becomes, the more likely the new learning will be long lasting. These are new connections that are formed by active reflection of ideas.

Effective teaching is not just about delivery of content; it also requires that students reflect on and process what is delivered. It is the student who needs to create these links.

Work with students to expand on the concept map by leading them towards contributing ideas and links.

Knowledge storage is not a passive sport. Students need to be thinking about how to recall and apply ideas to really store them in their brains.

Active recall strengthens understanding and memory. The more we access and utilise ideas, the easier it is to access them in the future.

If the group is sluggish, you could again increase dopamine by asking small groups to rank or arrange a series of related ideas in order of importance.

Then discuss concepts. Try to link students' contributions together. Once a student responds, add this to the visual concept map and ask another student to expand on or extend the ideas. This develops a collective map of ideas and also teaches students about how to take notes.

Information processing is about encouraging critical thinking.

Curating great learning experiences

Critical thinking

How teachers can encourage it	What students would be seen doing
• Open-ended questions • Spirit of inquiry and possibility • Essential questions	• Comparing, interpreting • Observing, summarising and classifying • Suggesting hypotheses • Taking decisions; creating; criticising and evaluating • Designing investigations • Identifying assumptions • Coding, gathering, and organising data • Applying principles to new situations

Then tie the experience together by consolidating. This is **Transfer** time and is best done by considering other applications for the new knowledge.

It is time to package the knowledge for storage and later use. This is the process of consolidating meaning so that knowledge can be used later.

Prompts like the following can be used:

- Think of three other uses for …
- Transform this knowledge into a poster/flow chart/mind map.
- Make a tape or podcast or create a model.
- Think of an analogy or metaphor.

Transfer is enhanced when students are asked to:

- Transform the information into another format
- Anticipate or predict where information could be used in another area
- Generate quizzes to test themselves on their retention next lesson
- Summarise the information
- Create a picture of the information
- Post information on intranet personal files
- Mind-map the information
- Create metaphors and analogies.

Never lose the last five minutes (it's not free time, it's transfer time).

Making learning "stick"

Effective learning requires focused input of information, processing to develop comprehension and understanding, as well as the capacity to retrieve and recall information (outputs). This is not a passive process that occurs without some planning and effort. Learning is not a spectator sport.

Small tweaks in the practices of most schools will make major improvements to the capacity of students to recall and utilise the knowledge they learn. Together these methods increase the durability of learning.

Unless we help students use these methods, they will not naturally utilise them. Generally students do not know what types of effort result in the best outcomes.

Curating great learning experiences

① Focus

Stephen Covey's great line "The main thing is to keep the main thing the main thing" is apt here. Learning suffers if students are overloaded by processing information that is not relevant to the knowledge and skills required for the task.

Anyone who has learned to play a musical instrument or drive a manual vehicle knows you can improve your ability to focus. Concentration is a skill that we can help all students acquire.

② Short, sharp intensives

The "Fortnite" generation are accustomed to brief immersive expeiences. Their concentration peaks for about 15 minutes and is followed by about 5 minutes of reflection.

Repetitions of learning experiences of this duration are most likely to be successful.

③ Multiple inputs

Learners of today have a wide variety of inputs to acquire new knowledge and skills. These include YouTube clips, massive open online courses (MOOCs), chapter quizzes, reading, online discussions, small group interactions, and skill acquisition workshops in addition to traditional class time.

Optimising the variety of inputs requires successfully monitoring and regulating one's own learning.

④ Making notes

Organising and transforming information helps the brain to process it. Arranging and creating notes on key ideas improves results. This is especially true when the notes contain: a learning objective, main points, the one main idea, and a visual linking the idea to similar concepts and differentiating it from dissimilar ideas (see outline in Chapter 9).

5. Spaced learning

Learning is significantly enhanced by inserting extra time in between repeated study sessions. "Drip-feeding" small amounts of information into brains over repeated learning times pays off.

This means schools should have some brief periods for the acquisition of new concepts that are repeated and built upon. These "high-rotation intensives" should be mixed with longer periods of time for delving into deep thinking and research.

6. Mixing it up (interleaving)

Brains love new information. It piques our curiosity and keeps us alert. Mixing up, or interleaving, different types of topics when studying improves retention. Scheduling dissimilar learning experiences after one another improves outcomes.

7. Flipped learning

This is where students study materials such as a video, some articles, or a filmed lecture related to a topic and class time is used to discuss and deepen their thinking.

8. Worked examples

Seeing examples of how a problem is solved, known as "worked examples", increases comprehension and outcomes.

Completion of similar examples by students familiarises them with problem-solving methods.

When students are learning new concepts, it is wise to lessen the emphasis on assessment and increase the use of worked examples.

9. Faded examples

After completing some worked examples, we can "fade" the instructions. Students are given partially worked-out examples and have to complete some of the solution steps.

The steps for fully worked examples are presented and then increasingly removed on subsequent exposures. This is particularly effective when we work backwards from the completion towards the beginning – for example, asking students to write a conclusion for an already written example essay.

Faded examples are at least as effective as worked examples and are often preferred by students.

10. Problem-based scenarios

After exposure to worked and faded examples, students are asked to apply their knowledge to a problem scenario. For example, after learning about diagnosing and troubleshooting malfunctions in electrical circuitry, students are then asked to apply a particular law to diagnose where the malfunction was occurring in an example circuit.

Students who receive alternating worked examples and problem-based scenarios significantly outperform those who receive only example problems. The ratio of one worked example to three problem-based scenarios is likely to produce the best performance

11. Practice in transfer of knowledge

Effective learners need to be able to access information from multiple sources, assess the validity of the information, process and integrate the knowledge in creative ways, and apply what they have learned to multiple settings.

12 Self-testing (memory retrieval)

Practising the retrieval of information from memory significantly enhances retention of that information. It is far more powerful than the methods used by many students – reading over their notes and summarising the knowledge.

Although the benefits of retrieval practice are well documented for memory-based tasks, these benefits are less likely to occur for more complex problem-solving tasks.

Retrieval practice study involves an initial opportunity to learn some information. This is followed by an opportunity to retrieve that information from memory.

The effects of retrieval are stronger when multiple retrieval opportunities are provided.

The power of retrieval is even more effective when followed by feedback that allows learners to correct their errors.

When practice is distributed over longer periods of time, students challenge themselves to reconstruct the information. This consolidates memory by establishing more meaningful and interconnected pathways in the brain. This dramatically increases the likelihood that the information will be accessible in different settings over time.

13 Distributed practice

Repeated practice experiences in recalling information increase the durability of that learning.

Ideally students would access a computerised program with mandatory quizzes that include worked examples, faded examples, multiple-choice questions, and problem-based scenarios. Feedback and progress charts would enable them to track their learning. For each problem, students could have the option of attempting to solve it, asking for a hint, or asking for the fully worked example.

14 Revision practice

Some schools expect their students to revise but fail to adequately teach them how to do this. My book *Unlocking Your Child's Genius* outlines a research-based method:

Study the entire subject or area of learning.

1. Devise a test to assess whether you understand it.
2. Look at the areas you need to work on.
3. Specifically study those areas.
4. Re-test.
5. Study the entire subject again.
6. Devise another test to assess whether you understood it.
7. Work specifically on the areas you don't understand.

Chapter 9
Extracting miraculously good marks

A lot of what happens in classrooms has nothing to do with improving marks. A clever teacher can save a lot of time by focusing on the activities that relate to improved outcomes for students. This chapter focuses on how to teach so that your students will learn and therefore get better results.

Meta-analyses can help with this. The following table identifies the key strategies and places them in order of the size of the effect and the percentile gain that can be expected by students of teachers who use this strategy.

Strategy	Average effect size	Percentile gain
Identifying similarities and differences	1.61	45 points
Summarising and note-taking	1.00	34
Reinforcing effort and providing recognition	0.80	29

Strategy	Average effect size	Percentile gain
Homework and practice	0.77	28
Non-linguistic presentations	0.75	27
Co-operative learning	0.73	27
Setting objectives and providing feedback	0.61	23
Generating and testing hypotheses	0.61	23
Cues, questions and advance organisers	0.59	22

You don't need to use all of these to make a substantial difference, but even focusing on the few most powerful ones will make a difference.

Summarising, note-taking, identifying similarities and differences

These are the most powerful strategies, and we can combine them into one nifty trick that will improve your students' marks.

1 Teach your students a note-taking system

This is the system I have researched and found effective. Students are asked to rule up pages with three main sections, as shown below. They first write their main notes in the area indicated, then at various points throughout the lesson you prompt them to write, "What is the one main idea?" Towards the end of the lesson, they are asked to transform the knowledge a third time into a Venn diagram highlighting how key concepts are similar and overlap and how others are different and distinct.

What is the main idea?	Main notes
Transform a third time – ideally into a Venn diagram	

Already in class they have transformed the same bit of knowledge into three different formats, increasing the retention of that knowledge. The problem is: it takes human beings 24 repetitions of anything to get to 80% of competence.

How do you get students to repeat anything 24 times? Let's show you how to give their memory a hand (see over the page).

2 Reinforcing effort and providing recognition

Feedback is a powerful motivator. Here are some ideas for increasing the amount of positive feedback you give:

- Place notes with positive comments on students' desks.
- Provide hit-and-run feedback through the "I noticed" method. For example, as you pass by a student, make a point of saying something like, "I noticed you know a lot about cars" or

GIVE YOUR MEMORY A HAND – ONE METHOD FOR INCREASING REPETITION

1. Ask students to cut out cardboard shapes of their hands. At the end of each topic or section of work, students are asked to give their memory a hand.

2. Each student or, if you prefer, small team of students cuts out a cardboard hand. On one side of the cardboard hand, they write the five most important pieces of knowledge, one on each finger or thumb. In the palm area, they either draw a Venn diagram or write a more detailed summary of the topic.

3. They then turn their hand over and write their name (or if it is a group of students, the group name), two questions that they can use to test their memory of the area, and one question that is really tricky. They then assign a points value to the tricky question.

4. Collect up the completed hands. At regular intervals throughout the year, shuffle and then distribute the hands with the questions facing upwards. People may get someone else's hand. Have students try to answer the questions before turning over the hand to check the answers. You can also use these in jeopardy types of games. This increases substantially the numbers of repetitions that students get of the same information.

5. Another way of summarising is to ask students to write down what they think the main point of the lesson was on a card and put their name on it. Collect up the cards. The next day, return the best summary cards to the students who wrote them and ask them to read them out aloud. This will also help you to know whether the information you so beautifully taught them was understood.

"I noticed you like drawing". Don't say any more. Sometimes with feedback less is more.

Research – homework and practice

Despite what some commentators will have you believe, homework from Grade 2 onwards is valuable. Research indicates it contributes to better results. Ideally, change the term "homework" into "research" or "skill reps" for your students.

The best homework is brief, interesting, and relevant. I like the idea of research sprints where you ask students to see how much they can do in 20 minutes. I find these sprints to be incredibly diagnostic. They will help you to identify your perfectionists and your procrastinators or put-it-off-for-another-day students.

Train students to turn homework into a regular spot in your classroom.

Tracking work handed in

An easy way of keeping track of turned-in assignments is to make sure that you get something from everyone. If they don't have their assignment, they must write "I did not hand in my assignment" and sign their name on a sheet of notebook paper. These statements are handed in and used as future proof. The key is to get something from every student. This will save you endless hours of looking for "lost" assignments.

Late work

Don't accept late work (unless there are REALLY exceptional circumstances). Make-up work actually punishes the teacher by having to mark and manage papers out of sequence. It also sends the wrong message to the students who do their work on time. Teachers who deduct points for each day of late work also create more work for themselves.

Research/homework hand-in day

Consider having all homework due on the same day. I'd suggest Wednesdays, so that you can aim to have it returned by Friday and have your weekends free of marking.

 Non-linguistic presentations

Posters, flow diagrams, mind maps, and charts – we live in a visual world. Routinely ask students in small groups to create a visual presentation of a piece of work. Consider scanning these and using them as a computer display.

Ask students to draw mathematical problems.

 Co-operative learning

The ability of teachers to use short, sharp group work with students increases student engagement, reduces behavioural problems, and increases academic outcomes. Do you need any more convincing?

Most classrooms are too passive. Being able to say to your students "Please stand up and go and explain to your shoe friend/area friend/arm-crossing friend/eye-tone friend (as explained in Chapter 1) three things you know about [whatever the current topic is] – you have three minutes" is incredibly powerful. It can be used as a standard practice that you put into place from day one. It can also be used to change a class where a malevolent storm is brewing.

Many students are used to controlling whom they mix with, and this allows cliques and factions to form in your class. I want you to be the boss of this gang!

Students will quickly learn that while their shoe friend/area friend/arm-crossing friend/eye-tone friend may not be one of their close friends, they only need to work together briefly before returning to their original seats.

As a rule of thumb, short, sharp group processing should be used about every 20 minutes in a class. Groups should only meet for a maximum of five minutes. As you go through the year, you will no doubt find that some group configurations work better than others, so no doubt they will be the ones that you use more frequently. Keep mixing them up though!

 Setting objectives and providing feedback

Setting objectives is a fantastic way to build confidence in a group. Just the very act of writing on the board "The aim of today's lesson is ..." improves outcomes.

The next step is to say: "Please write down three things you know about ... Then find your shoe friend/area friend/arm-crossing friend/eye-tone friend and develop a list of eight things. You have four minutes." This means that they are working, you can catch your breath, and the outcomes will be better.

 Generating and testing hypotheses

Probably the biggest inhibitor to students doing well is their fear that, if they get something wrong, they will appear stupid or shamed in some way. The best way I know to build a have-a-go culture in your classroom is to use Fermi questions.

Fermi questions

Enrico Fermi, an Italian physicist, was involved in the Los Alamos atomic bomb project and the development of quantum theory.

Fermi questions emphasise estimation, numerical reasoning, communicating in mathematics, and questioning skills. Students often believe that "word problems" have one exact answer and that the answer is derived in a unique manner. Fermi questions encourage multiple approaches, emphasise process rather than "the answer", and promote non-traditional problem-solving strategies.

A "typical" Fermi question is posed and solved below for illustrative purposes.

Fermi example: How many piano tuners are in Melbourne?

How might you figure out such a thing? Surely the number of piano tuners must in some way depend on the number of pianos. The number of pianos must connect in some way to the number of people in the area.

Approximately how many people are in Melbourne?
5,000,000.

Does every person own a piano?
No.

Would it be reasonable to assert that "Individuals don't tend to own pianos; families do"?
Yes.

About how many families are there in a city of 5 million people?
Perhaps there are 875,000 families in Melbourne.

Does every family own a piano?
No. Perhaps one out of every 20 does. That would mean there are about 43,750 pianos in Melbourne.

How many piano tuners are needed for 43,750 pianos?
Some people never get around to tuning their piano; some people tune their piano every month. If we assume that

"on the average" every piano gets tuned once a year, then there are 43,750 "piano tunings" every year.

How many piano tunings can one piano tuner do?
Let's assume that the average piano tuner can tune four pianos a day. Also assume that there are 200 working days per year. This means that every tuner can tune about 800 pianos per year.

How many piano tuners are needed in Melbourne?
The number of tuners is approximately 43,750/800 or 55 piano tuners.

Try it yourself

Use different assumptions for various factors. It is unlikely that you can justify an answer greater than a factor of 10 or smaller than a factor of 10 from the number originally obtained; that is to say, there are probably not more than 550 tuners and surely no less than 5. Thus, the answer obtained is good to within an "order of magnitude".

Fermi questions: some ideas for areas you might explore

1. What number of Ford Falcons is equal to the mass of the water in the swimming pool?
2. What is the mass in kilograms of all of the students in your school?
3. How many golf balls will fill a suitcase?
4. How many litres of petrol are used by cars each year in Australia?
5. How high would the stack reach if you piled one billion dollar bills in a single stack?
6. Approximately what fraction of the area of Australia is covered by automobiles?

7. How many hairs are on your head?
8. What is the weight of solid garbage thrown away by Australian families every year?
9. If your life earnings are paid to you at a certain rate per hour for every hour of your life, how much is your time worth?
10. How many cells are there in the human body?
11. How many individual frames of film are needed for a feature-length film? How long is such a film?
12. How many flat toothpicks would fit on the surface of a sheet of poster board?
13. How many pies will be eaten at AFL games during a one-year season?
14. How many revolutions will a wheel on the bus make during our school trip from Melbourne to Canberra?
15. How many minutes will be spent on the phone in a day by middle school students in Australia?
16. How many pizzas will be ordered in your state this year?

8 Cues, questions, and advance organisers

The number of students who don't do well in exams or tests because they get confused about what is wanted is mind-boggling. Advantage your students by helping them to understand and practise typical types of instructions. Discuss what they think is wanted and help them to clarify common terms.

Also prepare students for standardised tests in several ways. Prepare all tests and quizzes, including spelling, in a standardised format. With maths tests, require that the paper showing working and checking be turned in. That lets you see where mistakes are made for re-teaching purposes and teaches students to get in the habit of copying the problem down and checking it on the extra paper. Make the tests tricky, so students will realise that sometimes they must look more carefully than they first thought.

Assessment autopsies

Whenever you give a major test, consider giving students the opportunity of improving their scores by doing a test autopsy. They correct their mistakes and then write a half-page reflection on why they did so poorly and what they should have done differently. They earn a half point for each corrected answer. For example, if they got 15 out of 25 and did an autopsy correcting them all, their new score would be 20.

Aim to have all your students succeed. One way of doing this is outlined in Judy Willis's book, *Research-Based Strategies to Ignite Student Learning*. Judy asks her students to take a test correction paper in which they find in a textbook a problem that matches the problem they got wrong and then write that page number in their paper. She then asks students to write out what they should have done differently to solve the problem correctly. Students are then asked to solve the problem or calculation correctly, getting help if need be. After doing this, students can do a retest and obtain a higher mark. This allows students to obtain success and also to see the relationship between practice and success.

Gail Moncrieff from the Dandenong Ranges cluster of schools asks her students to create a rubric to assess their narratives.

	Above expected level	At expected level	Below expected level
Story/plot	• Distinctive style of writing • Creation of realistic, well-developed and described characters • Control of timing and sequence when events diverge • Maintenance of suspense, not giving the plot away • Uses knowledge of audience background to interest and engage audience • Moves away from predictable plot	• Engaging title • Developed characters with names • Enough supporting details • Own style of writing • Consideration of audience	• Predictable title • Briefly sketched characters • Re-written familiar plot • No consideration of audience

Extracting miraculously good marks

	Above expected level	At expected level	Below expected level
Structure	• Uses a range of strategies to plan, compose, revise and edit • Addition of text to add clarity • Full explanation in the conclusion with all the ends tied up • Selection of vocabulary for precise meaning	• Evidence of planning/ drafting • Organisation with orientation • Series of events in logical order • Complication, resolution/ conclusion • Appropriate length • Variety of simple and complex sentences	• No evidence of planning • Simple organisational structure – e.g., beginning, middle and end • Inappropriate length
Mechanics	• Extra features using illustration, appropriate fonts	• Correct spelling • Correct use of punctuation such as commas, exclamation marks, and quotation marks, to show sentence structure	• Handwriting not up to standard • High-frequency words misspelled • Little evidence of editing (meaning) and proofreading (spelling, punctuation, paragraphing etc.)

Anna Dollman also gives her students a list of main points about a topic they have learned. Students then rate their understanding of each from 1 (absolutely no idea) to 4 (understand it). Students with a "1" then find a student who has a "4" next to the same item and ask them to explain. Once a student understands it, they can upgrade their rating.

Some other ideas for improving student outcomes

- Use colours to highlight important messages.
- Write words on a soccer ball as a prompt for discussion – either answer for yourself or pass to someone who you think knows the answer.
- Ask students to summarise verbally.
- Work backwards – give a summary and then expand it back out.
- Ask students to develop "cheat sheets" (written summaries).
- Lead students through the task of summarising their notes, highlighting main ideas, and transforming the notes into different formats.
- Read a maths problem, then close the book and ask students to write down the problem in their own words.

Kristina Knudsen from Ceduna Area School has her students summarise important points in Gregorian chants.

Exams and essays

If you are teaching subjects that require students to write essays in exam situations, prepare them for this through practice.

Using sample essays and exam questions, ask students to analyse and discuss what the question requires the student to do. You'll be amazed how many students do poorly in exams not because they don't know the answer but because they don't know what the question is asking them to do. Then ask students to write up a plan for the answer including main points. Use this as a discussion point.

Also familiarise your students with common terms used in exam questions, such as those outlined below.

Terms often used in exam questions

Account for	Give a reason for something.
Analyse	Break a concept down into its component parts, or essential features, in order to examine relationships.
Analysis	An examination and identification of the components of a whole.
Assess	Determine the importance of something.
Calculate	Give a precise answer where there is only one possible solution.
Compare	Describe two situations, then present similarities and differences.
Define	Set out the meaning of a term. State precisely the meaning of a concept.
Describe	Give an account of something. An explanation is not required.
Discuss	Consider or examine. Make a detailed and careful investigation of two sides of an argument.
Distinguish	Make clear an understanding of similar terms.
Evaluate	Determine the significance of something.
Examine	Inspect closely.
Explain	Give the reason for or the cause of something. A description is not sufficient; an explanation of why something has occurred is required.

How?	By what means? In what way?
Illustrate	Show clearly, provide with visual material, and clarify by means of an example.
Outline	Give the important features of the topic.
To what extent?	Give a balanced judgement on a situation where there is some difference of view.
What?	Make something clearer.
Why?	Give reasons for the existence of something.

Do's and don'ts of essay writing

Do	Don't
• Answer the question given. • Plan your answer. • Analyse the question. • Brainstorm your answer. • Answer all parts of the question. • Define all key terms. • Divide into logically arranged paragraphs. • Include an introduction. • Develop points in full. • Include a conclusion that directly addresses the question. • Use examples and illustrations where appropriate. • Write legibly. • Ensure that each "sentence" really is a sentence. • Discriminate between relevant and irrelevant points.	• Ignore the key words. • Start writing before planning your answer. • Give too many ideas away in your first paragraph. • List points. • Ignore the later parts of the question. • Use slang or swear words.

You don't teach someone to hit a backhand in tennis by telling them not to hit a forehand. Think about it: how did you learn to swim, ride a bike, dance? The key is practise, practise, practise. Make sure your students have seen, used, and worked with information they will be assessed on at least three times before an assessment.

Before an exam, ask students to visualise a successful performance. Have a priming session with your class prior to assessments during which you ask students to name the things they think might be important to remember in a test or exam.

Chapter 10

Keeping your head when all about you are losing theirs

Running around like a busy adrenaline junkie might be a way to impress everyone else about how busy you are, but it's never going to be high in the fashion stakes.

It is not just overwork that robs teachers of their lives, nor is it just teaching the toughest, wildest bunch of ungrateful kids; it is guilt. There is a game played in most schools and in most organisations called, "I work harder than you do". The guilt police abound in many schools.

Many teachers work much longer than they need to for fear of someone saying archly, "You left early yesterday." Whoever said going home on time is slacking?

Either decide to please the guilt police or have a life. It's up to you. If someone says that they noticed you leaving early, I'd suggest that you say to them, as sweetly as possible, "Oh, you had to stay late, did you?"

There are commitments that you are allowed to have that do not involve your job. It is essential that you find some. Make sure also that some of these commitments do not involve alcohol. This is especially true for teachers in small country towns.

Here are a few suggestions on how to keep your head when all about you are losing theirs (and believe me there will be plenty of times you will feel like the only sane one in a madhouse!).

1 Avoid saying that you're "busy" or "not bad"

These are words of addiction and abuse in many parts of life. "How are you?" "Busy." "What have you been up too lately?" "Not much." "How are you today?" "Not bad."

Schools can be frantic and frenzied factories of busyness. It's really useful to act as if you have enough time. You have the same 168 hours every week that everyone else does. Act as if it is enough. So, when people ask how you are (which is often a question about whether you are as crazy and frantic as everyone else), smile back at them and say, "Great!" or "Never better, thanks!"

Start your own sanity schedule. The amount of work that a teacher takes home can seem endless. Designate different nights of the week for different purposes. For example, Monday and Wednesday could be for marking, Tuesday and Thursday could be for planning and organising upcoming units, Friday should be a no-work evening, and Sunday is the day to renew. Some people even go so far as to have Sunday as a no-phone day as well, though I know that will frighten the mobile addicts out there.

Consider having a 90-minute prep time every night so that you don't get behind in your work. Increase it to two hours if you have to prepare for a report. Subtract school meetings and in-service time from that 90 minutes to keep your life in balance.

② Eat a power diet for energy

Eat a high-protein, low-carbohydrate breakfast. Protein shakes with blueberries are great for energy. Keep a water bottle near you all day long, and have some low-GI snacks such as nuts or fruits throughout the day. I want you to be in good shape for the daiquiri and the dancing after work.

Be prepared to walk your students around the school grounds if you are needing a bit of fresh air.

③ Set some wildly audacious goals for yourself

People seem to thrive when they set some big-picture goals for themselves first. Whether it involves planning that next great holiday or a wild weekend away, or learning to draw or speak a new language, set something you can be passionate about. Fit work around these goals rather than the other way around.

In your diary put the big things in first.

Decide to live an extraordinary life. Doing so will help you to have a fantastic life and also make it much more likely you will be an extraordinary teacher.

There are four rules for extraordinary performance:

1. Anything is possible.
2. Nothing is easy.
3. When things are difficult, remember rule 1.
4. When things are easy, remember rule 2.

Increase your social connectedness

The sense of belonging that we have in our lives underpins our resilience. Make time for family, friends, and new pursuits. Join that sports club, choir, walking group, and class. Make sure life grabs you more than work does.

 Know you do morally compelling work

Teaching is one of the few professions that make a difference, not just to the next generation but to the generations that follow. Be proud of what you do. People are fond of enviously commenting about the holidays teachers get. Rather than getting heated and defensive, smile at them and say, "Yes, I really love those holidays. It was a great career choice!"

 Differentiate between true and fair-weather friends

In life and in workplaces there are fair-weather and true friends. Fair-weather friends aren't bad people. They hang out with you when the times are good, but if times get a bit tough, they disappear. Accept that this is just how it is.

True friends are those who stick with you through thick and thin. Try to be clear who is in each category, so your own expectations of people are reality based. This helps you to avoid being upset or disappointed in people.

Also keep an eye out for foul-weather friends. These are people who commiserate with others when there are troubles, but as soon as they cheer up, they head for the hills.

7. Sleep more

It is tempting in the maelstrom of life to get more work done by depriving yourself of sleep. Teaching is not a game you can play on less than all cylinders. You need all the sleep your body requires to function optimally.

Sleep deprivation will affect your moods and increase your vulnerability to stress. Guess what snappy and irritable teachers get back from their students? A living hell.

8. Be a reciprocator

While the ruthless characters often get the TV roles, being able to give as well as take leads to a happier life. Give to people. Show other staff and students that you are interested in them.

9. Know you are more than your thoughts

We all have days where we slump and groan and feel a bit flat. Know that these days will happen, and when they do, look behind the thoughts you are having to see if you can work out what has brought this about at this time.

Teaching is a high-energy, high-impact sport. Every so often, a student will push your buttons. At that moment, increase your level of self-awareness. Silently ask yourself questions like:

- I'm feeling tense; I wonder what that is about?
- Where in my body am I feeling this most strongly?
- Where in my body am I feeling ok?
- Where else in my life have I felt like this?

Sometimes removing the focus from action to self-awareness frees us up. It doesn't mean that the feelings of anger or upset or tension will immediately disappear, but it does equip you to deal more effectively with these feelings.

10 Remember life is short and precious

Teaching can be one of the best careers. It can be like running your own gang of bright, eager, enthusiastic kids. Make a pact with yourself to laugh outrageously at least 5 times a day and forgive yourself for 12 mistakes every day.

Chapter 11
What do I do when students ...

This chapter outlines some starter methods for teachers to consider when their students behave in specific ways.

What to do or say when students ask "What's the point of learning this?"

Say: "Good question. Let's see if we can work that out." Don't say: "I have to teach this" – it won't carry the day.

Restate the task and the reason why it might relate to broader goals.

Try to link to an area of student interest or learning strength.

Consider that anxiety might be a source of procrastination.

What to do or say when students ask "What do we have to do?"

Present instructions visually so the task is clear to all. Stressed students often don't focus on verbal instructions well.

Point to the display and read it out to them to help them to process it.

Ask them to nominate a partner to ask if they are unclear about what to do (then if they are both unclear, they raise your hands).

If students look confused, you may have to slow down; if they look bored, you may want to pick up the pace.

What to do or say when students come late to class

Having students come late to class is something that every teacher has to deal with. It interrupts the dynamic in the classroom. Deal with it before it becomes too big.

Outline your expectations at the beginning of the year. Make it clear how important it is to you that students arrive on time.

It's important to minimise the impact on those students who do arrive on time.

Ask the late student(s) to apologise, and let the other students explain the tasks on hand.

While it's not ideal to have someone enter the class late, it can provide an opportunity for other students. Ask the latecomer to join an existing group, preferably one with stronger students. This gives those students who have come on time the chance to explain the activity. It also gives you, the teacher, a chance to listen in and see how well the students have understood your instructions.

Being late doesn't necessarily mean that the student is a "bad learner". People think differently, so find which angle to approach the problem from for the individual.

There are a number of possible reasons why students arrive to class late. Considering which causes are at the root of the problem can help guide teachers to appropriate responses and strategies.

Understanding the reasons, however, does not require tolerating the behaviour.

Personalising discussions with students, either on a 1-to-1 basis or as a group, shows that you care and take their learning seriously. It can help students feel that there is someone who cares about their learning process.

Students might have a genuine reason for being late that they don't want to share with other members of the class.

What to do or say when students lack organisational skills or come unprepared for class

Disorganised students often have a hard time keeping track of their materials and using their time efficiently. Usually, multiple remedies will be needed as you teach these students to become organised.

Set up and stick to a routine

Establishing a daily routine will help disorganised students feel less frustrated and give them a sense of structure. Place this schedule in their take-home folder, tape it onto their desk, and post it in the classroom.

Research/homework

Require that homework/research goes home each night and is signed and returned every day. This will ensure that students are staying on track and will encourage students to be responsible for their belongings.

Enlist help from parents

Parent-teacher communication is essential when you are dealing with a student who has few organisational skills. Keep parents in the loop weekly by notifying them on their child's progress. Having parental support will show the student that you mean business, and that you and their parents are working together as a team to help them become self-sufficient.

Create checklists

Clearly define expectations by creating a checklist. This is truly the best tool to help students visually see what they need to accomplish and stay on track. Show students how to prioritise their list and check tasks off as they complete them.

Use memory aids

Memory aids are a great way to help disorganised students remember their tasks (see Making learning "stick", page 122) and class materials. Provide students with aids such as sticky notes, rubber bands, and timers. Have them tape checklists and class schedules to their folders and desks.

Enlist the help of a classmate to remind the disorganised student of important tasks and student expectations. Pair the student up with a responsible student that you can trust, to help them out when you are busy or absent.

Label and colour-code everything

The best way to keep students organised is to label and colour-code all of their materials. Students who lack organisational skills may feel overwhelmed when their materials are all over the place. Having specific colours for each subject will help students find assignments quickly and effortlessly.

All of these ideas can help transform your disorganised student into an organised one. These strategies will give students the tools and skills they need to manage their obligations and lead an organised life.

Disorganised students can drain so much time in a classroom. They waste their own time when they can't find supplies, don't come prepared, and have trouble focusing. Additionally, these students often cause other problems. When disorganised students can't focus on a lesson or on their own work, they often initiate disruptive behaviours that distract others.

What to do or say when students won't sit down/ get up out of their seat

Increase acknowledgement, proximity, and eye contact.

Ask the student for help – e.g., "While you are up, would you mind …" (remember that this is a request, not a demand!).

Consider a change of seating (check that they are not trying to get away from another student).

Use it as a reminder – e.g., "Thanks, Jett, you are right, people have been sitting for too long – everyone please stand up" or "Emily, you've read my thoughts – everyone stand up".

What to do or say when students are talkative

Whisper to them.

Figure out why they are chatty.

Having a structure really lays out the expectation that there's a time to talk and a time not to.

Break down today's learning targets into three essential questions. Those questions should be on the board when the students come in. Sometimes it's to work out a puzzle, imagine what the world would have been like before we knew it, answer quiz questions, interpret a picture, read a piece of information, or write some notes in their notebooks.

Structure those three things to cover the basics in the first question. That way, if there are some struggling students, they will get enough to participate in the lesson.

The next question asks them to draw a conclusion or infer something, usually from the first thing.

The third question just expands out further. Give them a few minutes to do these three things. It's brief. Then go into the main activity of the day.

Some students don't know how to be quiet and are so dependent on group work and working with a partner that they have almost forgotten how to think for themselves.

What to do or say when students swear

Confronting challenging kids when they have an audience will make them more rebellious.

Ask: "Are you ok? That's not like you. What's going on for you?"

Model politeness. Reduce the sense of threat.

Consider if there is something the student is trying to distract from, and if there is, why?

Set up with the student a predetermined signal to indicate when inappropriate language is used.

What to do or say when students make sexualised comments to you or other students

State that this is not appropriate. We treat people with respect here.

Consider sharing your concerns with parents.

Consider whether this student knows the difference between friendly and sleazy.

"I can see you are trying to be friendly, but there are better ways to do that."

What to do or say when students don't want to follow a process

Pretend that you are not speaking to them but to the whole class as you outline the task.

Move closer to them as you speak.

Arrange pairs or small groups.

What to do or say when a class is hard to settle

Use your "discipline spot".

When you have to make a disciplinary comment to the entire class, do it in this spot.

Never teach in this spot.

Move slowly and purposely towards this spot before speaking.

Don't talk too much – if you talk too much, tension dissolves. Fewer words are better.

Don't discuss consequences. This often leads to debate, which is not the real issue. The real issue is that there has been a disturbance, and you want it to stop so you can get on with your teaching.

Your goal is to regain the peaceful state before the disturbance.

What to do or say when students are shy

These students may score highly on standardised tests but rarely participate in classroom discussions. They are shy students and often hide behind their anxiety and fear of talking out loud in the classroom.

The causes are the fundamental two: nature and nurture. There is evidence that some people are born with a genetic predisposition for shyness.

If kids have good models, such as parents, teachers, or other significant adults who model effective communication, they are less likely to develop into shy people.

Try to have activities where everyone speaks to the person next to them.

What to do or say when students interrupt the class and other students learning

Acknowledge their comment, then tell them you will ask them to contribute soon.

Consider whether they are feeling they won't get heard any other way.

Silently count the number of times they have interrupted you, and then have a quiet conversation. "I don't know if you realise, but you have interrupted me X times today (or this week) – how do you feel when you get interrupted?"

Be specific

It's important to define for your students what interrupting is – because, believe it or not, more than a few won't know. Give examples using the specific interrupting behaviours you're seeing in your classroom.

Explain why it's wrong

Simply and directly explain why it's wrong to interrupt, why it's disruptive to learning, and why it isn't allowed in your classroom. Knowing the why of your expectations will always result in better buy-in from students.

Model what to do instead

Now show your students the required alternatives to interrupting. Show them the ease of raising one's hand, the politeness of waiting patiently for you, and how much more peaceful and conducive to learning it is without interruptions.

Reward those who do it right

Respond quickly to those who raise their hand and wait to be called on.

Don't respond to those who interrupt

If a student interrupts, calls out, or stands in front of you repeating your name, don't respond. Because, for every time you do, you create an avalanche of more of the same behaviour.

Enforce a consequence

Instead of responding to interruptions, or even reminding students to raise their hand, look them in the eye and say, "You have a warning" or whatever consequence your classroom management plan calls for.

Interrupting is unfair

Interrupting is like cutting in line; it isn't fair.

What to do or say when a student is disruptive

Change the pace of classroom activities: restructure situations and involve students in other activities that require active student participation and help them to refocus interest.

Remove distracting objects: collect the object that is competing with the teacher.

Boost your level of involvement: show interest in the student's work, thereby bringing the student back on task (walk over and check how work is going).

Redirect behaviour: refocus the student's attention, ask them to read, do a problem, or answer a question (treat the student as if they were paying attention).

Use non-punitive time out: ask the student if they would get a drink or invite them to run an errand or do a chore.

Encourage the appropriate behaviour of other students: make positive comments about other students' behaviour, which involves making good decisions.

Provide cues for expected behaviour. Use a cue that students understand: close the door, flick the lights, or even make a motion with your hands.

Stand closer to the disruptive student as you continue to teach the class.

What to do or say when students annoy or aggravate other students

Calmly explain what the student is doing wrong, specify what they should be doing, and ask them to do it.

Say: "I can see you are a people person, and I like that about you, and there are also times when I need you to work by yourself."

Agree on an activity to do while the student waits for assistance.

What can a teacher do if students just don't care?

Have high expectations for all your students.

Reinforce the message that in your class everyone gets smart.

Most students who say "I don't care" actually care deeply. They fear failing so much that they would prefer not to even try.

Let them know that you care and believe in them (even if they don't care right now).

What to do or say when students call out random silly things

Raise one hand. Model what they should do.

Do not reply verbally to them until they raise their hand.

Chapter 12
The best guerrilla tactic of them all

You always know when you are in the presence of a great teacher, because their eyes smile at you. What is behind those smiling eyes is a generosity of spirit. And what creates that is a deep sense of purpose.

Your vision and sense of purpose can be slippery customers. They give you grace and a big-hearted world to live in, but they can also sneak off and go missing at times when you need them most. The soul-deadening, dispiriting burden of deadlines (they are called "dead-lines" for a reason), to-do lists, and the driven expectation that you are always available and able to squeeze out more and more in less and less time and still bounce back smiling, drains us.

Every teacher has hollowed-out, empty days when their sense of making a difference disappears and they lose belief in their capacity to help their students effectively – days when the love of teaching evaporates. The best guerrilla tactic of them all is knowing how to come back from those days. Resilience is the happy knack of being able to bungy jump above the obstacles of life. Let's give you some strategies to achieve this.

While we should resist as many activities that zap our energy as we can, we can also shift our thinking in regard to time. Of all the resources you have at your disposal, time is the one resource that is not renewable. Prioritise your energies and allocate your time wisely.

Whenever you can, shift from "have to" to "get to". Instead of thinking I "have to" go to the shops/catch up with my friend/teach this class, and so on, tell yourself you "get to" do these things. In this way we can increase our appreciation and gratitude.

We sometimes associate the expression of purpose and satisfaction with big events such as birthdays and family gatherings, but it is more often found in the little moments of life – a great song, the smell of a home-cooked meal, sliding between fresh sheets, a smile, contact from a long-time friend, the aroma of a baby's head, or even the knowing acknowledgement from a tricky student. The magic of life is held in these fleeting moments, and we need to be careful not to miss them.

You will have met some work colleagues, other teachers, who have lost contact with their love of teaching. Their spirit has been crushed by their work demands. Resentment has a grip on them. Cynicism and bitterness are always barren places to be. All teachers work hard. Wise teachers take the time to recover, refresh, and renew.

I'm sure you've also spoken with a young person who seems empty and hollowed out by life. Their dreams and hopes have been stifled. Talking with them is like spending time with a much older, world-weary person. When you guide them towards their strengths, they look at you warily and dismissively. They have been too wounded by life to trust easily. Trust takes time and consistency. When you stick by them and continue practising gratitude rather than rushing them to be something other than what they are capable of being, slowly, gently they unfold and become who they truly can be.

I'm sure you've met other young people who are "armoured up". They have a full arsenal of emotional weaponry on show. If they could, they would spit in your eye just in case it entered your mind to spit at them first. Everything and everyone is considered suspicious and probably dangerous until proven otherwise. You know that if they are put in the hands of the wrong person, an entire alphabet of diagnostic terms will be thrown at them (and none of them are likely to help them!). These young people may not have much in their lives to feel grateful about, but they do know loyalty when they see it. So much of great teaching is about creating and curating quality relationships.

Then of course there are the people you rely on most – your friends and loved ones. Loving gratitude benefits everyone you know when you practise it. When you feel lucky to know the people in your life, it is better than winning any lottery, prize, or accolade. When you intentionally take on feeling lucky to know the people who come into your orbit, you shift your world.

There are also aspects of yourself that have been suppressed or starved of nourishment and recognition. Some of your early hopes and dreams were killed off through harsh words and disapproval by judgemental others. As a result, parts of you have been surviving on handed-down crumbs and leftovers rather receiving the sustenance they deserve. The philosopher Nietzsche once relabelled all of his "worst" and most disapproved-of aspects as his very best attributes. What a liberation of energy!

There are parts of your inner world that haven't felt the warmth of acknowledgement for years. When we fail to be kind to ourselves, we banish aspects of who we are and become dislocated and diminished. Applying kindness and appreciation to the entirety of yourself, the neglected as well as the valued parts of yourself, completes you. There are unrealised strengths within you that are yet to be fulfilled. Life is an improvisational art, and it is also a banquet of possibilities. Try to unpack those potentials that are within you. Give them the opportunity to fully breathe and live.

Michelangelo was once asked what he did for a living. His response wasn't to say he was a sculptor. Instead, he replied that his job was to remove the excess marble to reveal the beauty of the figure within. At its very best, teaching is just like that.

Helping young people to discover their strengths and treasures within themselves requires teachers to have three things:

1. Good ears
2. Big heart
3. Great spirit.

"Good ears" involves listening beyond the words. Hearing the fears, dreams, and hopes of your students, their parents, and your colleagues increases your compassion and kindness. No one can be as cool as today's young people feel they need to pretend to be. Behind their screens, camouflage, and cover jobs, they are all scaredy-cats, especially the ones who act toughest. One of the great lessons I have learned after many years of doing therapy with people is that if you sit with someone for long enough and listen cleanly and clearly, they will find an answer to their troubles.

Big-heartedness is a great antidote for a time-poor, reductionist world. We are beginning to celebrate diversity rather than uniformity. We are starting to know that we all have different brains and can be smart in different ways. The basis of comparisons between students is looking shakier. And yet we still cling in schools to outmoded notions and definitions of what success is and what education is truly about.

Hopefully schools will find the courage to redefine themselves. In the meantime, none of your colleagues have enough time or energy, none of your students truly feel supported to become all that they can be, and none of their parents feel that they are doing a perfectly good job of raising their kids. When a system results in everyone feeling that they are failing in some way, big-heartedness and gratitude open up a space to create the antidote.

Great spirit involves living well. One of the best gifts teachers can give their students (and parents can give their children) is to show them how to live a great life. This is more often modelled rather than taught. Developing a great spirit requires living life richly, absorbing the best that is on offer and using it to understand the great themes and dilemmas that face us all while also appreciating the nuances of difference between people. This is true cultural literacy.

Albert Einstein once said, "There are only two ways to live your life. One is as though nothing is a miracle. The other is as though everything is a miracle."

Which life will you choose?

www.ingramcontent.com/pod-product-compliance
Lightning Source LLC
Chambersburg PA
CBHW011955090526
44590CB00024B/3795